Epstein

Learning to Live Again

A Guide for the Recovering Addict

Learning to Live Again

Again

A Guide for the Recovering Addict

Jill S./Brian S.

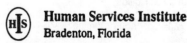

Human Services Institute
Bradenton, Florida

TAB BOOKS

Blue Ridge Summit, PA

FIRST EDITION
FIRST PRINTING

Library of Congress Cataloging-in-Publication Data

Jill S., 1953-
   Learning to live again : a guide for the recovering addict / by
Jill S. and Brian S.
     p. cm.
   Includes index.
   ISBN 0-8306-3743-5
   1. Narcotic addicts—Rehabilitation. I. Brian S. 1947-
II. Title.
RC564.29.J55 1991   90-27847
616.86′03—dc20   CIP

TAB Books offers software for sale. For information and a catalog, please
contact TAB Software Department, Blue Ridge Summit, PA 17294-0850.

    The publication of this material does not imply affiliation with nor approval
or endorsement from Alcoholics Anonymous World Services, Inc., Narcotics
Anonymous World Services, Inc. or any other Twelve-Step Fellowship.

Development Editor: Lee Marvin Joiner, Ph.D.
Copy Editors: Pat Hammond and Pat Holliday
Cover Design: Lori E. Schlosser
Cover Photograph: Susan Riley, Harrisonburg, Virgina

Questions regarding the content of this book should be addressed to:

Human Services Institute, Inc.
P.O. Box 14610
Bradenton, FL 34280

Dedication . . .

I dedicate this book to three beautiful people: Mr. Bob Smith, Mr. Frederick Jewett, and Mrs. Mary Nelson. These three individuals, all very close to me, died while I was writing this book. In dealing with these losses, I proved to myself that I never have to rely upon drugs again to cope with life—*one day at a time*. Although I felt intense pain from each loss, I did not find it necessary to use any mind-altering substance. The principles of recovery in this book work!

Contents

Acknowledgments . . .

My heartfelt thanks to all those friends who made this work possible:

Fred and Clara Jewett for critical reading, initial editing, encouragement and "gentle" chiding . . .

Richard and Mary-Alice Jafolla, coauthors of *Nourishing the Life Force* (Unity Books), for further editing and proofreading: thank you for believing in this project . . .

Ruth Skinner for being my *Master Mind* partner . . .

Edward T. for holding my emotions together, and teaching me tolerance . . .

the God *of my understanding* for providing the patience and love which the ideas in this book have helped me discover.

Thank you all!

Authors' Notes . . .

If you're wondering who Jill S. and Brian S. are, we want to tell you in as gentle a way as we can that at the beginning of recovery such questions are natural, but they are also meaningless. In this book we speak as one; the *"I"* says it best. *Drug addition is a problem each of us deals with individually and personally.* Drugs didn't ask questions about our position in life and our vital statistics. In recovery, we don't either.

I do not practice anonymity for effect. Sobriety and clean-time are in direct relationship to my practicing the Twelve Steps and Twelve Traditions of both Alcoholics Anonymous (A.A.) and Narcotics (N.A.) and accepting that, although in my essence I may be a unique expression of God, in my addiction I am just like every other alcoholic or addict. I know that now, but once, like every other addict, I denied it. The denial centered on my conviction that *"Nobody's had these feelings before."* I truly believed my feelings and insecurities were unique—special.

A moment of truth came after attending a few twenty-four-hour recovery meetings. I learned that all addicts have felt my inner conflicts. When I realized this and stopped thinking that my addiction was different, the recovery process began. We addicts all experience our moment of truth. There is only one way to avoid it—death.

The programs of Narcotics Anonymous (N.A.) and Alcoholics Anonymous (A.A.) are responsible for my recovery. Their Twelve Steps are its heart, and their Twelve Traditions its backbone. Had there been a Cocaine Anonymous meeting available in my small hometown in Florida, I would have been in the front row. Had there been Heroin, Marijuana, Speed, LSD, Barbiturate, Crack, or Valium Anonymous meetings, I would have been active in each.

My addiction was a hell inside a hell. Recovery was slow and shaky at first. But now my life is better. In the depths of my addiction, I never thought it could be this good. I'm so proud of myself that it is difficult for me not to brag! I have a lifestyle that is exciting yet peaceful, a lifestyle that is both rewarding and fulfilling. Thanks to the Twelve-Step program I have regained my dignity and I have a love affair with life that is getting better *one day at a time.*

I would like very much to hear readers' ideas, thoughts, criticisms, or compliments, and I will reply (anonymously) to each letter. Please write to:

Jill S. or Brian S.
c/o Human Services Institute
4301 32nd Street West #C8
Bradenton, Florida 34205

Introduction . . .

Every addict eventually stops using drugs. Some are alive when it happens.

"Why me?"

"Why me?" may be a question you're asking yourself as you hold this book. It's a question I ask too. I ask it differently today than I did on my first drug-free day; but I still ask, "Why me?"

A good friend of mine stopped doing drugs two weeks after I did, using many of the same recovery ideas you'll find in this book. He started to advise me when my thinking got out of line. Oddly enough, I found myself accepting his advice and listening with an open mind. It was probably because of the humorous way he always presented his advice. Pinocchio had Jiminy Cricket for an advisor, and I had this fun-loving friend, a friend with two weeks less drug-free time than I.

I wish my Jiminy Cricket was still alive. Tears well up in remembrance; I still miss this companion who died from his drug addiction. The advice so freely given to me, and which I value even today, was not practiced by my friend. Today, I wish I'd known what I've since learned about remaining drug-free. I wish I could have given my friend what he needed, instead of just taking. Now, I share with you, the reader, what I wish I could tell him. That's, "Why me?"

Many addicts become drug-free for short periods of time, either on their own or with the help of others. Unfortunately, not enough of them are taught how to *remain* drug free. This book explains what it takes to stop using drugs and to stay stopped. Whether you are an addict, a relative or friend of an addict, or just someone who wants to know more about recovery, the material presented here will help demystify addiction and recovery. If you are a recovering addict, the ideas in this book will help you achieve long-lasting sobriety.

The tools of recovery are simple. The complication, if any, is with the addict. *Recovery is a simple program for complicated people.* A newcomer to drug recovery is a ball of confused energy demanding quick answers and short explanations. This book is a blessing for the newly arrived, rapid-thinking *gimme-some-answers-now* drug addict. Highlighting many essential ideas from Twelve-Step recovery programs, it is easy to read and understand.

Besides recovering addicts and their families, who should read this book? It should be read by anyone who is concerned about how to counteract addiction. Regardless of their position or educational background, readers will find this book invaluable in fighting the problem that is eating away at our nation, and slowly destroying our beautiful world —drug addiction!

PART ONE . . .

For the Recovering Addict

1 . . .

Sliding Down . . .

The Stages of Addiction

Many addicts who have stopped using eventually return to drugs because they remember only the good times. Unless the addict learns how to retain the pain of the drug, keeping it fresh in memory, the drug probably will return to finish the destruction.

Drug addiction is a progressive illness, and its predictable symptoms have been identified. "Social using" slowly becomes "problem using" and finally progresses to the uncontrolled addiction to a specific drug. Loss-of-control usually occurs about the same time abusive behavior begins. Drug users become short-tempered and start to abuse others verbally or physically. They seem to lose their sense of humor and, although they may still be "enjoying" their drug, their reason for taking it has become a

NEED, as opposed to a WANT. This phase has been called *the crucial phase*.

People who show signs of problem using will sometimes temporarily stop taking a drug. Momentarily drug-free and with a renewed sense of power, they deceive themselves by thinking, *"See, I knew I could stop!"* The discomfort of withdrawing from the drug is quickly forgotten and the addict soon starts all over again experimenting with less potent drugs. Such users inevitably find themselves back where they started: addicted and despairing.

When people who have stopped using drugs begin again, they slowly relapse into the same despair they were trying to overcome. They soon find that their addictive disease has progressed (gotten worse), even while no drugs were being used. Why is this? For one thing, during just one year of abstinence the body ages. We're all a minute older than we were just a minute ago. Also, because of certain facts of body chemistry that are associated with addiction, a relapse usually picks up momentum rapidly—as if the abuse had never stopped at all.

Addiction is a progressive illness, but you will find that recovery is also progressive. Specific levels or stages can be identified in both addiction and recovery. The "Progression of Drug Addiction" chart (*Figure 1*, below) should help you identify how far you have advanced in your addiction. A similar chart, showing the stages of recovery, appears in Chapter Two.

Figure 1. The Downward Progression of Addiction

↓ INTRODUCTION TO DRUGS

 ↓ SOCIAL USING

  ↓ BUYING AND STASHING

   ↓ MISSING COMMITMENTS

    ↓ LOSS OF INTERESTS AND WILLPOWER

     ↓ USING ALONE—PARANOIA SETS IN

      ↓ SEX, WORK & MONEY PROBLEMS

       ↓ MORALLY AND FINANCIALLY RUINED

       ↓ DOWN FOR THE COUNT

INSANITY, JAILS, DEATH · OR RECOVERY

Each stage in the progression of addiction will be explained below. As these stages are explained, compare them to your own behavior.

THREE BIG QUESTIONS

Not all individuals experience identical symptoms of addiction, nor do they necessarily walk through them in the exact order that they are presented here. Further, there is no timetable for this progression. Some addicts have gone through a cycle of alternating many different types of drugs, and some used only one or two before their enemy was made known. It may take some people years to get *sick and tired of being sick and tired*, but for others, it can happen quickly—perhaps within a year of drug abuse, or even less.

As you begin to review your own "nonmagical mystery tour," try to avoid thinking about the ways you are NOT like others, and instead try to IDEN-TIFY with them. Identify with the inner feelings that these stages represent for you. This advice applies both to the stages of addiction and of recovery. Though your life history may be different than other addicts', your feelings may be very similar. To begin to have a better understanding of your own addictive problem, ask yourself three big questions.

- How and when did my addiction begin?

- Did I progress gradually toward addiction or jump immediately from social usage into problem usage?

- At what points did I stop, relapse, or deceive myself?

INTRODUCTION TO DRUGS

If you are like most addicts you probably were introduced to a drug when your feeling of self-worth was at a low level. The chemical may have been a socially accepted one, such as beer or another alcoholic beverage, or it might have been a little marijuana or a tranquilizer. Whatever the drug, it probably lowered your inhibitions (your natural restraints or controls) and helped you feel that you fit in, that you "belonged." This might have started those "no cares, no problems" type of effects . . . yes, and it felt good. More than likely, it also produced or increased a stubbornness within you. *Have you realized yet that you can't reach anymore the highs you used to find?*

SOCIAL USING

Now you may have a tendency to use more around other people, with a show-off attitude which may have hatched at this level, too. Deep inside, you just want to be accepted by friends; you just want to be wanted. Your drug inspires you with newfound courage and strength, yet a little more of the drug is needed for each buzz. This "little more" is occurring more often than you dare to admit to others—and especially to yourself. This "little more" is occurring so slowly, in fact that it's barely noticed.

Your attitudes toward your own drug use may have gradually developed into a lack of interest or concern (apathy). You say "*I don't care . . .*" at this stage of abuse. The drug is CUNNING, BAFFLING, AND POWERFUL.

BUYING AND STASHING

The drug's stimulating, or perhaps relaxing effects, depending upon which drug is being abused, tend to create power thoughts. It feels like you are doing the impossible; like you're challenging the world to a duel and winning! "Big-time" and unachievable goals begin to clutter your mind. Illusions or false impressions of your life and what you can do with it are created by the drug. Sometimes it works in reverse. You dream of no goals at all; you become completely crippled by your apathy. Reality is slowly leaving and this state feels more and more comfortable. You say, "*Just leave me alone . . ..*"

But something else is leaving that *doesn't* feel comfortable: your self-worth, your self-esteem. Your innocent enthusiasm for life, your hunger for knowledge, your just plain "*I care . . .*" attitudes—these are also leaving. Even sex may not be important now—not as important as the drug, that is.

A supply or "stash" appears to spawn some comfort. Of course, the more drugs that are purchased, the more money is required. It's hard work to keep up.

BREAKING COMMITMENTS

You start to change friends, preferring those who will stay up all night and do drugs with you, those who will help you justify your progressing addiction. You begin avoiding your responsibilities, rationalizing your poor choices the same way your newfound friends do. Your job, or school, just doesn't seem as important as before. You say to yourself, *"Maybe I'll skip work (school) today . . . besides, I'm tired."*

Then you begin to think maybe you could buy extra dope and deal a little to your old friends who don't do as much as your new ones, or to other associates. Your concern for the drug is starting to become constant. Your obsessive behavior (fully explained in Chapter Three) is unfolding without you being aware of it.

LOSS OF INTERESTS AND WILLPOWER

About now, you begin to lose interest in the things you used to do—the things you once enjoyed. Although a friend or family member may warn you that you've gone overboard with your drug use, you begin saying, and probably believe, things like *"I can handle it"* or *"I can quit anytime I want to."*

You've now progressed to where you don't stop using until the drug is all gone. You don't seem able to stash it away for later anymore. The "crucial phase" of progression is now setting in. Periods of loneliness are occurring, and it seems that nobody understands your situation. The "helter-skelter" feeling has begun, and a certain amount of unmanageability is evident in your life, too.

USING ALONE—PARANOIA SETS IN

At this stage, one drug may begin to take priority over all others. This is now your drug of choice. Still, you may occasionally give a little away to relieve your guilt over becoming addicted. *"Giving a little away"* doesn't happen too often, because now you're sick and you need more. Paranoid thoughts and fears of running out of your drug of choice set in. When your original supply is used up, you begin to spend all your time and energy searching for more of the drug.

Social events just don't fit into your lifestyle any more, unless drugs are available . . . or even a specific type of drug! You begin to feel physically and mentally spent, especially if there are no drugs available. *"Fears of impending doom"* (called the F.I.D.S.) have set in, meaning: *"I don't know what's going to happen to me. I don't know when, where, why, or how it's going to occur, but something is definitely going to happen and it's going to be bad; yeah, real bad."* Tremendous fear and terror rise up within you and the loneliness is even worse than before.

PROBLEMS WITH SEX, WORK, AND MONEY

Guilt is snowballing. Your decision-making capacity is gone. Your promises continually fall short. Your efforts to quit the drug once and for all fail. Your self-esteem has fallen so low that you need the drug consistently to escape from yourself.

By this time, most addicts have found that their ability to perform sexually when high has decreased drastically. Even your arousal, your interest in sex itself, is obscured by the effects of the drug. Drugs can truly become more powerful than even the desire for sex.

Persistent remorse and guilt regarding money—how much of it you spend on drugs and what you will do to get it—are increasing. Addiction, the disease of denial, is now the emperor of your life and you've become a human slave to the drug itself. You think, *"Oh God, please help me . . ."*

MORALLY AND FINANCIALLY RUINED

The financial disaster that now exists or awaits, compounded by the loss of respect from family and friends, is creating even more hopeless thoughts. Your bizarre and unmanageable behavior and judgments are causing you to think of taking a rest for a while someplace—anyplace—or even contemplating suicide. You start to filter messages like: *"I'm just tired . . . tired of fighting, tired of running, tired of the lies. Just sick and tired."* But also, you know the score that tells you: *"You can't use drugs and you can't quit—and you're going to die."*

DOWN FOR THE COUNT

From the now-evident physical deterioration and possibly drug overdoses, you are convinced that you're powerless over the drug. You realize, with what little sense is left, that you've lost the fight. The drug that eats away at your physical, emotional, and spiritual fiber—cocaine, prescription medication, designer drugs, heroin, marijuana, crack, or booze—has won.

Family, friends, job responsibilities or school commitments—none of these matter any longer. You are in a cage with a wild monkey on your back. The monkey doesn't fight fair, and you lose . . . except now you can open the cage door and be free! You can open your mind and learn how to be content, and to enjoy life, perhaps for the first time.

2 . . .

Looking Up . . .

The Stages of Recovery

This chapter is about "the light at the end of the tunnel"—the stages of recovery. An addict can't THINK his or her way into good living; instead, he or she must LIVE a certain way into good thinking.

Shortly before seeking help for my drug problem, I witnessed my friend's child, approximately eight years of age, playing with two other children. When I was eight, we would pretend we were characters from television, from comic books, or even heroes from the movies. These three kids were playing "The Drug Dealer."

Another thing I noticed about my friend's child was how he would imitate our defiant and sarcastic mannerisms. One day, while driving through a toll booth with my friend and his family, the person in the booth said pleasantly, "Have a nice day." The child I'd witnessed pretending to be a drug dealer immediately shot back loudly, "Don't tell me what to do!" Although I laughed along with the other adults present, I felt very uncomfortable inside. Something was wrong—very wrong. Recently I learned that this same child had been arrested on felony charges.

How to let go of old ideas, and how recovery works is what this chapter will begin to explain. The difference between thinking about becoming drug-free and living in the freedom of recovery will be made clear. There's no blame—blame is wasted energy. You too may think, "Don't tell me what to do!" Okay, I won't. Read and decide for yourself if you want to have a nice day—if you want to see and feel the light at the end of the tunnel.

Sometime during the life of every recovering alcoholic and drug addict, a crisis of overwhelming proportions occurred that proved to be a turning point. When alcoholics and addicts hit bottom—when they are just plain sick of the lives they are living—recovery begins.

Only people who have lived through the depths of the hell of drug addiction have known those unique "lows," those states of despair, emptiness, fear, and loneliness. Only those tarnished souls will gravitate to that same extreme of a natural high. The serene peaceful fulfillments of recovery are composed of:

- Helping others

- Losing your fears and paranoia through the Twelve Steps of recovery

- Having an important purpose in life

- No longer feeling empty and alone

Recovery is like an entirely new life. The "you" leaves and is replaced with a Godsend of the most powerful two letters an addict in recovery will ever hear: "*WE.*" The "WE" takes over now. Thank God! You're safe now. We're in this together, and it is going to be okay from here on.

In recovery we have feelings of tranquility, freedom, and excitement. It seems as if we're so far above everything that we're looking down at heaven itself. How does this work? How does it happen? How do we get started? **H. O. W.** is how. **H. O. W.** means:

Honesty

Open-mindedness

Willingness

Rather than staying in a cage with a monkey scratching at us, ending up either insane, confined to jail, or dead, we can completely surrender to the illness of drug addiction and ask *Honestly* for help. Here is where the **H.O.W.** begins to go to work. Don't worry about the Open-mindedness and Willingness;

you've already got a start on these. Only an open-minded and willing person would have read this far. Hope is born! As you study the tools of recovery, start believing that they will work, and they will.[1]

The levels, or stages, of recovery shown in Figure 2 are guideposts on the road to recovery from addiction. Note your progress on the chart as you follow your recovery program. Also, frequently reevaluate your personal commitment regarding these stages. An honest reexamination reinforces your admission and acceptance of your problem, and reaffirms your desire to build a solid foundation for a clean and sober life.

---

[1]Note: This book isn't meant to be read like a novel, read once and then discarded. Repetition will bring bonuses never thought possible. Please read it, or parts of it, again and again. You won't be sorry!

Figure 2. The Upward Progression of Recovery

BEYOND YOUR WILDEST IMAGINATION

↑ ENJOY ONGOING RECOVERY

↑ CLEAN UP

↑ SET PRIORITIES IN ORDER

↑ ESTABLISH SPIRITUAL VALUES

↑ FEEL INNER CONTENTMENT

↑ ADMIT POWERLESSNESS

↑ ATTEND 12-STEP MEETINGS

↑ LEARN MORE ABOUT ADDICTION

↑ IMPROVE PHYSICALLY

↑ RESOLVE TO STOP TAKING ALL DRUGS

↑ RECOGNIZE THE PROBLEM

RECOGNIZE THE PROBLEM

The fact that you are reading this book shows that you suspect you have a problem with drugs. Perhaps in desperation you have called out for help, but nobody answered. You haven't known where to turn, but you have an honest desire for someone, somehow, to help you. Some of you, on the other hand, may be in such extreme denial—your illness concealed so well from yourself—that you are attempting recovery only because others have forced you to seek help. You are fortunate, because help has come before you are permanently "covered up" by your illness—in the ground, that is.

The following guidelines will help you to recognize and understand your dependence and sustain your motivation. Remember, anyone can get off drugs; it is staying off them that can be tricky. If you have an honest desire for help with your addiction, you have made the first and biggest step on the road UP toward recovery. Reexamine this desire daily. Do you really want a life of sobriety more than the kind of life you've been living? Do you want sobriety or just to be free of the nagging from other people? Do you really want to stay out of that cage?

In later chapters, you will be shown how to overcome the obsessive thoughts that may occur in early recovery. Read on and keep moving progressively upward on the chart.

RESOLVE TO STOP TAKING ALL DRUGS

We must stop using all chemicals in any form—but *"Just for Today."* Somehow we know, deep within ourselves, that total abstinence is essential for recovery. There is no chemical solution to life's problems. Since our systems have come to expect and demand drugs regularly, predictable withdrawal symptoms occur when we stop taking these chemicals. A detoxification unit may have already helped this process along, but many chemicals that have been abused are stored up in the fat cells (many within the brain itself), and only time will completely remove them. Although we try to minimize the physical and mental discomforts of early abstinence, we must expect a little discomfort for a time.

Don't be alarmed if months later into recovery an effect of certain drugs begins to surface again momentarily. This is just the releasing or cleansing of chemical residues stored in the fat cells. Cigarette smoking often provokes this effect—as though the nicotine were loaded with marijuana. The effect quickly passes, though. Some people become irritated if this occurs, because they've grown to enjoy their drug-free thinking and hate the drug's returning influence, even though temporary. If this happens later in recovery, don't panic. Remember, *"This too shall pass."*

Telephone conversations with drug-free people already in recovery will help overcome your difficulties, fears, loneliness, and other discomforts and confusions. Check the yellow pages or newspapers for

Narcotics Anonymous hotline numbers. Other groups that will help are Cocaine Anonymous and even Alcoholics Anonymous.[2]

When calling one of these hotlines, understand that the anonymous person on the other end of the telephone line has thought what you've thought, felt what you've felt, and will help you head in a new direction. Ask them how they've handled their fears, loneliness, and despair. Ask them how they keep the monkey off their back. Soon, if not already, you'll realize that you can't do this alone. *"Reach out!"*

IMPROVE PHYSICALLY

Your physical recovery has already begun. It started the moment you stopped taking the drug itself. After being sober and clean awhile, you begin to realize the amount of abuse and damage that active drug addiction inflicted on your body. For some in recovery, normal sleep returns slowly. Regular exercise helps return our sleep patterns to normal. Nutritious meals help, too.

Start your own daily exercise program. Keep it simple, though. Walking is fine exercise, as are

---

[2]Note: Family members and friends of drug addicts have their own support group meetings and hotlines, and they're also confidential (see Chapter Thirteen, A Guide to Codependency). Check out these local support groups. Their help is free.

cycling, swimming, and aerobics. But check with your physician first, and begin slowly. *"Easy Does It."*

You probably don't feel your best yet, but gradually, you're improving. A person new to recovery, a newcomer, needs to start eating balanced meals. For some, the appetite returns very slowly. To speed up recovery, a daily multiple vitamin might help; but again, be sure to check with your physician first. A "stress tab" (vitamins B-complex and C) taken a couple of times a day has been known to help many in early recovery. Shop for these at your local pharmacy or health-food store and ask the store manager for brochures to read on detoxifying the body. (See Chapter Eight for more information about nutrition.)

Your thinking will become clearer as the effects of regular exercise, sleep, and normal eating habits begin to take hold. Remember, you must become physically healthy first. As your physical health improves, your mental health follows suit. Then your spiritual side begins to improve. With spiritual improvement, your sense of humor is restored, your well-being is mended, your outlook on life improves, and you begin to like yourself and others more. One way to think of the often misunderstood word "spiritual" is: *"Spiritual" is full of life, full of love, full of energy.*

So, all these combined—physical, mental, and spiritual improvements—help us to develop into a whole person. For some of us, this healthy development is happening for the first time.

Please do not treat your physical improvement lightly. Exercising and eating well are a necessity, so be consistent. Make exercise and good eating daily habits. Include six glasses of water per day. Midday rests, or afternoon naps, are also a good idea.

You start paying more attention to daily hygiene; regular warm showers or baths are not only hygienic but soothing. Wearing clean clothes begins to make us feel extra good, too. Don't worry about some of the oddities that many of us develop early in recovery, such as brushing our teeth several times a day, taking several showers or baths, or other harmless idiosyncrasies. For some of us, it is as though we're trying to make up for lost times of our lives. Go ahead and do these as often as you like; you've done stranger things than this before.

Avoid "regular" coffee in the evenings, and you'll sleep better. Remember, too, that while most colas contain caffeine, caffeine-free and sugar-free formulas are available for evening consumption. Some recovering addicts swear by keeping a Narcotics Anonymous or Alcoholics Anonymous book on the pillow next to them (or use the reviewing of this book) to drift off to sleep with. This way, the last thoughts before heading off to dreamland are about recovery.

LEARN MORE ABOUT ADDICTION

Along our road of recovery, we learned that drug addiction and alcoholism are a disease. Knowing that the *American Medical Association* and the *World*

Health Organization regard alcoholism and addiction to drugs as a disease, however, isn't enough to remove the guilt, embarrassment, and shame for some of us. These confused feelings have hampered us from getting straight in the past and can get in the way again. It is a fact that addiction is not a matter of weak character or lack of willpower. Our disease has affected us physically, mentally, and spiritually, and so we've become genuinely sick.

Although addiction is a treatable illness, there isn't a cure for it. It can be arrested, though. Arresting the disease means "to stop its progress," and it is the only way to fight this terminal illness. Although our disease is progressive and terminal, it can be arrested no matter how long it has been active. If we have to have a terminal disease, this is one we can live with because we can stop its deadly progress.

You cannot arrest the disease of addiction by yourself. To look at this disease in a half-believing (*"I can handle it . . ."*), foggy manner will only send you back to the hell you thought you'd left behind. Begin to check out some local meetings of Narcotics Anonymous, Cocaine Anonymous, and even Alcoholics Anonymous. Try both "open discussion" and "speaker" meetings to help you to understand which meetings are best for your recovery program.

For a few meetings, just sit in the back and listen to the other addicts who've been clean and sober for months or years. As they share their relatively contented lives with each other, and discuss their daily problems, try to identify with them. Comparing yourself with others, with thoughts like "*I'm not like that person in any way at all,*" is being closed-minded. All drug addicts are alike in one way or another. If nothing else, we are all defiant and rebellious; the word "stubborn" sums it up.

If an addict is singing (so to speak) "*I did it my way . . .*" then he's singing "*the loser's national anthem.*" We've tried the "my way" trip before, and it didn't work. In fact, it almost killed us. Now let's try it the way millions of other recovering people are finding solutions. Notice how they depend upon each other's knowledge.

ATTEND TWELVE-STEP RECOVERY MEETINGS

Through attending meetings, you immediately find out that you're not as apart from others as you once thought. The shared feelings of past loneliness from other addicts at these meetings, and listening to them discuss their former and even present fears, helps you begin to overcome your own discomforts. You begin to discover that you're no longer alone. Then, as you start to share, it's as though a "*hat of honesty*" slowly comes to rest on your head. With the confidentiality that you feel within these meeting rooms almost instantly, embarrassment disappears. The confusion that has been raging within you begins to subside. The guilt begins to melt, and the gratitude starts to increase and strengthen. "*Finally, I've found people who understand me; who accept me, as I am.*"

Sharing ourselves with others is central to recovery from addiction. Sharing helps to stimulate our honest admission of the disease of addiction, reinforcing and maintaining our desire for recovery by helping others. Newcomers to Twelve-Step meetings both give and receive. They receive encouragement, acceptance, and support. And they provide a chance for others to give, too.

ADMIT POWERLESSNESS

When we finally recognize and admit that we are powerless over all drugs, that we cannot control our use of them anymore, we feel a great sense of relief. We've known for some time that if we drink, we'll eventually be drunk. And the pot or the pills just don't seem to have the same effect they once did. Whether we shoot it, snort it, smoke it, drink it, or even sit in it, the influence is now different—and we know it. It just doesn't have the same kick as before.

Any addictive substance that either revs-up our mind or sedates our thinking is dangerous—and we know how dangerous. A total surrender and admission of powerlessness over drugs, *just for today*, will begin to open the door to self-esteem because part of self-esteem is being honest with ourselves. With a daily review of our surrender, new horizons will appear almost immediately. Honesty is power. But unless honesty is combined with ACCEPTANCE, it will weaken.

FEEL INNER CONTENTMENT

We feel disturbed when someone or something seems unacceptable to us. When we can learn to recognize that the world is the way it is and that it won't be changed by us, or anyone else, regardless of how much we wish it would, it is the beginning of acceptance. Then we learn to shift our attention from what we think is wrong with the world to what needs changing within ourselves. This we can control.

We do not stay sober and clean unless we accept our addiction. And, we do not find any happiness or contentment unless we accept life on life's terms. In other words, *the position of God is filled!* In the past, we thought we were the Director of this drama of life. Now we realize that we aren't. God is the Director, and we're his agents. It's time to look outside ourselves for direction.

ESTABLISH SPIRITUAL VALUES

Millions of drug addicts and alcoholics who have sought and accepted spiritual help have recovered. Many were at the depths of despair and hopelessness, but their openness to spiritual ideas pulled them through.

There is a principle that is a bar against all information, which is proof against all arguments and which cannot fail to keep a man in everlasting ignorance—that principle is contempt prior to investigation. - Herbert Spencer

Ever since you can remember, you've been told that the North Pole exists. You no more doubt this than the fact that apple pie is a dessert. Then again, you've probably never seen the North Pole. Maybe it really doesn't exist. Maybe a scientist just made it up. Maybe you've been lied to all these years.

Many of the things we believe and do in recovery involve faith and believing in something we can't see, touch, or measure. Forgiveness, gratitude, and love cannot be analyzed under a microscope, yet nobody denies that these qualities exist in life. We in recovery experience these qualities at different times and see their results repeatedly—especially at Twelve-Step meetings.

So, do you think that the North Pole exists, even though you can't see it? Yes, of course it is there. And so is there a Higher Power, though some of us deny its existence—at first. Some reasons for this denial are: not believing ourselves to be worthy, guilt, and self-centeredness. But obstacles like these will all disappear as our recovery progresses.

Having looked into the depths of despair, we find it easier to find a Higher Power, to find a God of our understanding, and "*change the analyzing to utilizing.*" Some have even simplified their spiritual directions to the acronym K.I.S.S.: Keep It Simple Spiritually. And hold onto the openmindedness.

SET PRIORITIES IN ORDER

By attending Twelve-Step meetings we come to realize that we weren't really that good at being that bad. Besides, *"We're not bad people trying to get good, we're sick people trying to get well."* Focus on that quote. Read it again and again until you absorb the truth of it. No, we didn't ask for this disease. But we're sure doing something about it.

In recovery, we *"stick with the winners,"* realizing that some newcomers may have their priorities confused. There seems to be a "head instinct" that we follow and we just know who "the winners" are. We've also found it best if the men stick with the men, and the women stick with the women in early recovery. It is more successful this way. We all need to keep our priorities in order. If the men think of the women as their sisters, and the women think of the men as their brothers, there will be more addicts staying alive and drug-free. You'll have plenty of time for romance later, but we need to get to know who we are, first—*"first things first."*

Try to avoid minimizing the threat of premature sexual affairs by joking about them and pushing the issue aside as if it's really not that important. It's a critical area of concern for addicts in early recovery! Why is this so important? The best answer is the power of obsessions. Always be aware of how danger-ous obsessions are for addicts—and sexual involve-ments often become yet another obsession, like the drugs themselves, consuming all thought. If it feels good, we want more of it—regardless of what it is.

I've witnessed many relapses that resulted from premature sexual involvements between men and women in drug addiction recovery programs. Let me give you an example, a story about two beautiful people who got their wires crossed about priorities while trying to make their ninety meetings in ninety days.

Paul and Maria met at the meetings, and both were within a few weeks of being equal in drug-free time. Both had made remarkable progress . . . until they started seeing each other outside of the meeting rooms. They'd both been warned of the dangers of early recovery romances, but defiantly ignored the advice. They got an apartment together.

For a while, I thought I was going to witness the one-in-a-million early-recovery relationship that worked. Yet, all to soon, Paul relapsed with booze and became violent, beating Maria severely. Attempting to defend herself, Maria reached for a kitchen knife while trying to get away from Paul, only to have her own throat cut by the same knife.

Paul had completely lost control of himself from the booze, as many relapsers do, and struck out at anything in sight. Their apartment looked as if a hurricane had destroyed it. Although Maria lived, she spent weeks in the hospital and has an ugly scar. Paul is still in jail.

Early emotional relationships just don't work. If you're already married or involved in a serious relationship, consider some extra counseling. If your mate refuses to go with you, go alone. Believe me, it will help. If you feel this matter is out-of-control, or too difficult to talk about, please write to *Sexaholics Anonymous*, P.O. Box 300, Simi Valley, CA 93062, telephone (805) 581-3343. It's confidential.

CLEAN UP

In recovery, we begin to take better care of ourselves, practicing good hygiene. We move toward developing dignity within by improving our outward appearance. Starting the day with a shower or a bath seems to give us a clearer field of thought, and topping off with a clean set of clothes causes our feeling of self-worth to improve. Brushing our teeth more often than before just makes us feel better. It's like saying, *"Yeah, I'm okay with myself, today; I'm worth it."* Slowly we begin to clean up our language, too. Some say, "You are what you eat," and others interpret, "You are what you speak." Change yourself, yes! But don't try to change others, and be careful not to judge them. Remember, *"live and let live!"*

ENJOY ONGOING RECOVERY

Some of us never seemed to complete anything, and when we did, we didn't seem to want it anymore. Did you ever have that feeling? Many of us have. But these feelings and thoughts do not apply to meetings. Live *"one day at a time"* is advice you will come to love and cling to in recovery. It just fits into place for all of us and erases many fears. Don't concern yourself with wondering whether you'll be sober and clean in a year any more than you're concerned about what will be happening thirty years from now. The "One Day at a Time" way of thinking will add up before you know it, keeping worry and fear from dominating you. "*Just for today*" we don't use or abuse. And that's all that's important. Sobriety and clean time can be likened to a plant. If we nurture and care for the plant daily, it will not only live, but grow. If we neglect it, it will die.

BEYOND YOUR WILDEST IMAGINATION

The following statements are promises that will be kept—guarantees—if you keep going to Twelve-Step meetings.

You will be clean, sober, and happy.

Your guilt over the past will leave.

You will forgive yourself and others.

You will find peace and serenity.

You will work well with other suffering addicts.

Your "poor me's" of self-pity will leave.

You will learn to find yourself by forgetting yourself.

Your fears and loneliness will disappear.

You will develop a good, positive attitude and outlook on life, filled with gratitude and humor.

You will realize the love and beauty of your Higher Power, and find the strength you've always sought.

3 . . .

Obsessions
and Triggers . . .

Once drugs are out of the body, the problem rests in the mind. This chapter explains how to get rid of obsessive thoughts and drug-craving triggers.

Once you have been detoxed and drugs are out of your body, the physical need for them ceases to be a problem. Your body itself does not desire the drug anymore. It's all in the mind now. The obsessions, or cravings, are what you must deal with.

The mind is the source of one of the addict's biggest troubles . . . a never-ending desire to obtain relief from confusion or emotional pain. This is one of the addict's strongest appetites. Some addicts express an intolerance for emotional pain and uncertainty with statements like "*I just don't fit in*" or "*I don't belong anywhere.*" Often, an inability to handle emotional pain is masked by declarations of boredom. Grounded in fear and rooted in selfishness, our longing for a pain-free existence is nonetheless real.

While we were living in the active drug culture, filling this "empty gap"—this emotional cavity—became the focal point of our lives, our reason for existing. Everything else seemed secondary. We believed it was the drug itself we sought, but it wasn't. We desperately wanted relief from the confusion, release from the emotional pain—something to fill that hollow feeling inside.

Now, in early recovery, our feelings tend to swing up and down (illustrated by the "Normal and Abnormal" charts in the next chapter). Our dissatisfaction, impatience, and dis-EASE can mount from just simple everyday events, such as shaving, going to work, punching the clock, or traffic delays. If we're five minutes late, we get angry with ourselves and short-tempered with others. It's as though a twisted perfectionism is guiding us. This attitude doesn't allow for any mistakes at all.

Intolerance (a fancy word for being close-minded and pushing away the beliefs and opinions of others) and not accepting what's happening in the world around us at any given moment can trigger dangerous obsessions. Also, allowing immature, *I want it now* attitudes to control one's daily thought patterns—in other words, impatience—invite obsessions to return, too. The qualities of patience and tolerance, which are vital in recovery, are not the addict's strongest points, so both need immediate attention. Delay can be dangerous.

One way to find relief from life's unavoidable confusions and frustrations is to *sleep on it*. For many, sleep gives an almost immediate relief from the day's misunderstandings. "I think I'll sleep on it," some say, is a way to postpone a problem. Another example of finding temporary relief from confusion, for some, is yoga. Many people achieve serenity and clarity through meditation, religious rituals, and even strict diets. Millions of people worldwide are obtaining relief from confusion and emotional pain by going to Twelve-Step meetings. Instead of running to a cocktail lounge after work, or hiding at home with a drug, these anonymous people use each other's energies to fill that "empty gap" *one-day-at-a-time*.

In our progressive recovery, we develop a sense of humor that permits us to make mistakes without punishing ourselves. But meanwhile, our tolerance level needs close watching. Developing tolerance for frustration, confusion, and the uncertainties of life is essential for recovery. *"Honesty gets us sober and clean, but it is tolerance that keeps us that way."*

OBSESSIONS

An obsession is an idea that overcomes all other ideas, a thought that overcomes all other thoughts.

Have you ever experienced, on a Tuesday or Wednesday, for example, your thoughts being almost completely dominated by what Friday's paycheck will do for you? Maybe in the past you blocked out the day's problems by thinking about which drug you would purchase with Friday's paycheck. Maybe you spent most of the day thinking about this just to pass the time away—*"a thought that overcomes all other thoughts."* Addicts tend to avoid reality by unleashing and even glamorizing these obsessive thoughts about drugs. When obsessions grab hold, we don't think the drug all the way through, back into the hell that it brought us.

Those Who Forget Their Pain Are Doomed to Repeat It

There are a few in recovery who have difficulty remembering how painful their drug addiction was, and these few will need help in learning how to *"retain the pain."* The cunning, baffling, and powerful aspects of drugs can sometimes sneak up on us, causing us to *conveniently* forget the pain that they took us through on our last escapade. We lie to ourselves, saying *"It'll be different this time; this time I'll be able to handle it."* Of course, it's worse than the time before.

At our Twelve-Step recovery meetings, both the newcomers and the teachers keep this fact alive and in front of us. "The teachers" are those who come occasionally to meetings and have relapses, but live long enough to make it back to a meeting to tell the rest of us that it was worse than before.

A Mental Videotape

Okay, so what can we do to overcome obsessions? Beginning today, right now, do yourself a favor and develop a five- to ten-second mental videotape of the pain that drugs have brought you. Create this imaginary videotape to fight any deceitful thoughts of the drug's supposed benefits. When creating your imaginary videotape, don't forget the thoughts and feelings you had when you were actively drugging:

- Paranoia
- Loneliness
- Guilt
- Fear
- Physical exhaustion
- Suicidal thoughts

For some of us there was the thought of "taking a rest for a while . . . maybe in a hospital, or anyplace that would care for us." Also, can you remember your last vomiting episode? What about jail? No? Maybe not yet. Then what about "the yets." Add those to your personal videotape, too.

Turn your videotape on when you think an obsession is beginning. Honestly think the drug all the way through. Then, go to a meeting—maybe even two—that day. Go and get your batteries charged up.

TRIGGERS

When we concentrate on something, it seems to get bigger. In recovery, we need to stop concentrating on the problem or else it will seem to get bigger. Instead, focus on the solution. This positive approach downplays the problem and all the negatives that go with it.

One way to focus on the solution instead of the problem is to get rid of your drug-related stuff. We need to "change playgrounds and playmates" as is strongly suggested at the meetings. Let me give you an excellent example of this one before going any further.

A couple of years before finally finding ongoing recovery from drug addiction, I attended an Alcoholics Anonymous meeting, feeling there was something wrong with me . . . always trying to find enjoyment, motivation, relaxation, or a sense of direction in life through drinking booze. I knew right down to my inner core that there was another way to lead my life, I just wasn't sure how.

The topic of discussion in that first meeting was, you guessed it, "*changing playgrounds and playmates.*" After listening to almost everyone else in the room make what I know today to be excellent suggestions, I was asked to comment. Unfortunately, I put on my "*pretending I know all the answers*" hat, and started motoring my mouth.

I said, "We're not living in the dark ages, and if any one of us wants to sit in a bar room and drink a cola, we should go right ahead and do it. And as for changing playmates, my friends have nothing to do with how much I drink and don't drink, and that includes whatever else I'm using to catch a buzz." Nobody in the room criticized me or corrected me, but I'm sure today that some of them knew I wasn't finished using yet. They were right.

Don't misunderstand me. I did want to get away from the imprisonment of needing booze or drugs to cope with life. I guess because I pretended to know all the answers at that first meeting, I just wasn't teachable at that time. *"Don't tell me what to do"* was still the attitude controlling me.

We need not only to *"change playgrounds and playmates"* but also to change playthings! It's a good idea to have another person more experienced in recovery accompany you on this detail. This involves cleaning out your junk drawers, the trunk of your car, your school locker, your desk at work, or any other places where rolling papers, beer cans, and general drug-related stuff may be lying around. Get rid of all of it—at home, at work, at school. This way, a few days or even weeks later, there will be no tempting reminders.

Another positive thing to do, at least for a while, is to get into the habit of changing radio stations so you aren't constantly hearing songs that get the drug thinking going again. Everyone had a favorite song or two while they were drugging. Hearing these favorites can cause thoughts of drugs to surge back. So, just change the radio station or the tape. Don't allow yourself to subconsciously focus on the drug.

REACH OUT!

We addicts in recovery have found that to combat obsessions and cravings we need help from another addict or alcoholic who has walked through these shrewd obsessions. Call. Ask for help! Remember, we can't do it alone.

Have you ever witnessed a young child who is being stubborn, demanding that he be left alone to continue doing whatever it is he's attempting? *"Let me do it. Let me. Let me!"* is the sort of urgent phrase we hear as the child refuses help.

This defiant, stubborn nature is always with us in the background, ready to push away much-needed criticism, advice, or help. How often have we said, *"I can handle it"* or *"I don't need your help"*—even though it's usually untrue? A phony and childlike sense of pride and rebellion is at the wheel.

"Letting go of our old ideas," a phrase we often hear in recovery, means taking command, pushing the "rebel without a cause" away, and replacing that driver with a teachable, open-minded person who truly desires to stay drug-free. There's nothing wrong in reaching out to another in recovery who has more answers than you, nor does it make you weak, or less of a person. No, it does just the opposite. Who are

the really smart people in the world? They are the highly educated ones, the engineers, physicists, economists and so on, right? These people become capable only by reaching out to other people who had the answers or knew how to get them: teachers, professors, and other experts. Reaching out works. So let go of the rebel and become teachable.

Drug use continues in vicious circles, we know that. We've all been there. We've all experienced the *"round and round we go, where we stop, nobody knows"* crap. Some of us have begged for sleep after days of sleeplessness, and other times have woken up in places we couldn't remember going to. A few of us have lost our cars from the night before, not remembering where we parked last, and a few of us have taken another's car (or other items), blinded and confused by the drug's crazy commands and directions.

Taking drug addiction to its extreme, it's only a matter of time before we invite death—the sort of death that a person dies not only physically, but mentally and spiritually. The body, mind, and inner spirit decay through loneliness and fears never known by most people; drugs eventually suffocate us.

What most of us didn't realize is that there are three choices that every drug addict eventually faces:

Recovery

Insanity

Death

Your choice is RECOVERY.

Recovery—getting our feet firmly planted and stopping those crazy thoughts, feelings, and actions—replaces going to jails or "wacky wards." I've spent time in a mental ward, and believe me, there is a lot of screaming during the night. It is not a nice place to be—nor is a jail.

Other proven ideas for how to make your recovery easier, more successful, and more fulfilling appear in later chapters. Why not try them? The bars and drug houses aren't going anywhere. Give it your all. What have you got to lose?

4 . . .

What is
Normal? . . .

What is normal? The illustrations in this chapter will show what emotional balance in recovery looks like.

My worst subject in school was math, and I know that graphs and charts can be confusing. But the horizontal line in Figure 3 represents a healthy, or "normal" level of functioning. (For years I confused "horizontal" with "vertical"—just remember that horizontal means even with the horizon, where the land or sea meets the sky, or a line going from left to right.) The line below illustrates a normal level—not too high or too low, a comfortable place to be.

Figure 3. Healthy or "Normal" Feelings

High

Normal ————————————————————————————————

Low

When we soar above this line emotionally, being
excited or stimulated, we must come back down.
When we come back down we usually go below the
line before coming back to normal. It's like throwing
a tennis ball up into the air at the beach; when it
comes down and hits the water, it goes below the
surface a little way before it returns to the surface.
In the next illustration (Figure 4), the horizontal line
again illustrates a normal level. The zigzag line is an
example of where drugs take a person.

Figure 4. What Drugs Do to Feelings

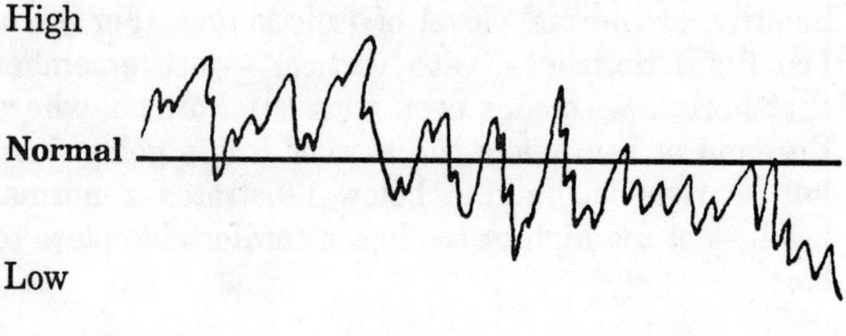

High

Normal ————————————————————————————————

Low

In drug addiction, the higher we go the lower we will fall before returning to normal. But, have you noticed that your early high just isn't available anymore, no matter how often you try? Consider the tennis ball again: if left in the water for too long, it becomes water-logged and lies suspended below the level of the surface.

Depending upon which drug is used, the effect might have been to create more energy or faster thinking; or it may have induced feelings of calm and relaxation, of being carefree. But eventually the drug doesn't return you to where it once took your mind and body. In fact, it doesn't even return you to a normal level any more. Instead, it takes you to a low only addicts experience, and an inner pain that words cannot describe. After a long period of abusing drugs, you just can't seem to return to normal thinking or feeling any more. The fears and the internal loneliness have dipped you into a hell very few understand. Some of those unbearable lows tempt death itself, and death often wins. Once a ball is waterlogged, it's shot, and will only sink itself.

The next illustration, Figure 5, below, shows what happens in early recovery. We tend still to go up and down, but not to the extremes we experienced while doing drugs. We don't have as much of a rebound to recover from. Think of a beach ball, instead of a tennis ball. The beach ball cannot be thrown as high as the tennis ball, but when it does fall into the water, it barely sinks beneath the surface, quickly rebounding to a normal level. Those terrible lows don't exist anymore, and there isn't the risk of becoming waterlogged . . . staying below normal emotionally.

Figure 5. Early Recovery Feelings

High

Normal

Low

Remember that recovery is progressive, too. An example is how you're feeling right now. Notice how you've stopped shaking, and you're feeling a little better. Well, next week you're going to feel even better; next month better yet; and a year from now, many parts of your life will be much enriched. Don't think that recovery just stops. Progressive recovery means *"advancing step-by-step."*

There's a common saying at Twelve-Step meetings that we all should remember: *"This too shall pass."* And it always does. Notice the up-and-down, swirling or rolling movement in Figure 5. Don't think of yourself as abnormal when your emotions tend to flow like this illustration, especially in early recovery. Most people in early recovery have mood swings, but they usually level out after eating something or exercising. Another practice that helps is to talk with other recovering addicts. You're not the only one who's experienced mood swings, so when they occur reach out and call someone.

The last illustration (Figure 6) shows what will eventually happen in recovery. "Not too high"—being rid of those racy, crazy thoughts—and "not too low"—without guilt and despair. Even those draining self-pitying and self-defeating thoughts and feelings will be gone. A calm comes over you that is like a permanent smile inside. It's like not reacting to others' negative actions and feelings, and just accepting everything and everybody the way they are—realizing that everything is the way it is supposed to be. Everything!

Figure 6. Later Recovery Feelings

High

Normal

Low

This last level of recovery can be compared to that beach ball just floating along smoothly. Not too high, not too low. That's the feeling recovery is all about: avoiding the alarming issues of excitement (which I confused with insanity for the first year of my recovery) and vamped-out stimulation, as well as the deep lows of depression from having gone too high and crashed down. Are you through bouncing up and down yet?

This feeling of serenity will grow as time passes in recovery, though there'll even be moments in early recovery when you will experience it. It does appear that the more meetings you attend, the quicker you cultivate an inner peace of mind. For most of us, this calm, smooth feeling of just floating along the top of the water is refreshing, relaxing, and desperately needed after being tossed up and down for so long. But please, don't confuse it with boredom! It's more like a peaceful feeling of the mind being comfortable and without confusions and misunderstandings. For many of us, it's feeling as though we fit in, wherever we go. Belonging!

5 . . .

Three

Newcomer Essentials . . .

There are three actions essential to successful recovery from drug addiction: get a sponsor, join a home group, and attend 90 meetings in 90 days.

How does a newcomer to recovery handle problems without using drugs? Whom do you talk to about thoughts and feelings that have been suppressed for years while you used drugs? Who will listen to a newcomer's daily complaints, confused thoughts and feelings about family members, work, or school? *"Please God, I don't want to take drugs anymore—but I'm dying inside. Is there anybody who will help me?"* Yes! Your sponsor will!

GET A SPONSOR

"Sponsor" is the name for a recovering Twelve-Step member who has been down the same road you've taken, but has come back. A sponsor may wear different clothes, but his or her feelings and thoughts were once identical with yours. Our lifestyles may be different, both now and before recovery, but the solutions we draw from each other are essentially the same. If you're a musician, you don't need a musician for a sponsor. If you're a physician, you don't need a physician for a sponsor. As one congressman in recovery joked: *"I came to you people for help and you gave me a house painter for a sponsor! I'm running your country and making important decisions, but this house painter is suddenly my advisor. Hmm!"*

It is best if men sponsor men, and women sponsor women. This keeps priorities in order. Besides, it's easier at this time to communicate your inner feelings and conflicts with someone of your own sex.

Qualities of a Sponsor

Getting a sponsor is not something optional in recovery. Sponsorship is absolutely crucial to long-term sobriety and clean time, and you'll need to find yours soon. What you are looking for in a sponsor are both the *quality* of the person's sobriety and the *quantity* (length of time in recovery). The length of time the person has been sponsoring newcomers is important, too. Someone who is new to sponsoring might be right on the button with helping a newcomer, but then again an inexperienced sponsor might try to help by trial-and-error.

Finding Your Sponsor

Begin with temporary sponsorship, also called a "contact friend." This is usually a thirty-day trial period in which another recovering drug addict helps the newcomer as he or she searches for the right person to fill the role of permanent sponsor. Some newcomers, however, find a stable member immediately. A "stable member" is someone who has fulfilled all of the Twelve Steps and is experienced in working with others. An excellent way to find the right sponsor is to bring up the topic of sponsorship at a Twelve-Step meeting. Then listen!

After going to meetings for almost a week, I'd heard enough about this sponsorship stuff to realize that I would have to get one if I was going to be doing what I should to stay sober. So one evening, I asked a person to sponsor me and was told, *"Yes, no problem. Oh, and by the way, once a week we'll go to a meeting together,"* and the time and place was agreed upon.

Now this went on for about a month, and I saw my sponsor once a week when we attended this meeting together. Other nights, I went to meetings by myself or with another newcomer. I talked with my sponsor only once a week, and very briefly at that.

One night, just before going to the meeting with my sponsor, an older person with a big, friendly smile asked my sponsor, "So where are you going tonight?"

"Huh? Oh, to (such and such) meeting with (a finger pointed to me with my name)."

"Oh, I see. Well, maybe one of these days you'll smarten up and get back to the step meeting." And then this friendly person laughed aloud and walked away, waving to us both.

I immediately took offense at the way this person talked to my sponsor and said, "Who the hell was that?" My sponsor quickly answered with a smile, "Oh, that's my sponsor. Don't pay any attention."

Well, I'm sure it wasn't meant in the way that I took it, but I couldn't get that message out of my head. That older, warm-hearted person had mentioned something that I hadn't heard of yet: "step meeting." Yes, the steps were being discussed at different meetings that I attended, but an ongoing step meeting was "where those serious people go," as I'd heard people say. Serious about their recovery, yes!

Anyway, I later asked this older person to sponsor me—even though I already had a sponsor. I'd heard the person speak one night the following week; the humor, assertiveness, and honesty impressed me, and I wanted some of it to rub off on me. The night I asked him to sponsor me, the person said, "I don't know. I won't just sponsor anyone. There are a few stipulations I'll need to explain to you, and if you still want me to sponsor you after you hear them, fine. If not, then that's fine too."

The sparkling eyes and lovable smile were somewhat hard for me to look at (my eye contact probably wasn't too good yet), but nevertheless, I still felt comfortable with the person as we sat down. It was explained to me that I would need to go to the ongoing Twelve-Step meeting "every week, without fail. I don't care if you've got the flu, I want you sitting there. Eventually, these steps will not only make sense to you, but you'll be eating, sleeping, and living them." Immediately I thought the person was being a little too demanding, but the smiles and love that almost oozed out of this person were overwhelming.

"Now the second thing I want you to do is call me every day, because I don't just want to share the bad days with you, I want to share the good ones, too." At that point, I began to feel warm all over. Here was a complete stranger wanting to share the good, the bad, and the ugly with me!

When finally I was asked, "Now, do you still really want me to be your sponsor?" I almost shouted "Yes!" Somehow, I knew that I was going to be safe. I knew I'd found my guide, my mentor in life.

Relying On Your Sponsor

After finding a sponsor, ask if you can call and check in daily. Most sponsors will request this anyway. Also, ask what is a convenient time of day to do this. Of course, whenever a problem arises—day or night—be sure to call your sponsor immediately. Slowly, with this daily contact, a bond will develop and you'll let your sponsor know who you are. Eventually, a special trust and confidence will develop between you. Each day the conversations will get a little longer and a little more detailed. Remember, however, call your sponsor at least once a day, especially early in recovery.

Is One Sponsor Enough?

What happens when your sponsor isn't available? Should you have more than one? Having more than one sponsor can work for some, but it's not suggested. The danger is that when a sponsor tells a newcomer he should do something that seems too hard or disagreeable, the newcomer's rebellious or defiant nature may make him turn to others for softer solutions. Newcomers have been known to keep calling other "sponsors" until one of them says what the newcomer wants to hear—instead of needs to hear. *"Stick with one main sponsor"* is good advice.

This doesn't mean that there won't be times when you will need an alternate sponsor. For instance, your sponsor might be away on vacation or at work. If you have problems to talk about, they often can't wait. This is a time when you will need another option. Your sponsor will be glad to help you arrange with someone else in the program to be your "alternate sponsor" during those times. The alternate sponsor also should be someone who is experienced in sponsoring others. The other important thing is to plan this in advance.

Get a sponsor! Don't deny yourself the compassion, understanding, guidance, love, and direction you'll receive. But do remember the sponsor isn't perfect. He or she just has a few more solutions than the newcomer.[3]

JOIN A HOME GROUP

Chances are, you didn't care for every bar you went to or the company of all the drug addicts that you met, either. The ones you didn't like, you probably stayed away from. Something similar may occur with the Twelve-Step meetings you're beginning to attend. If you don't like a particular meeting, go to another one. However, there will be one meeting that you will feel more comfortable attending. Don't bother trying to figure out why, just *join that group*! You do this by asking before, during, or after the meeting: "Who is the secretary of this group?" and signing on with that person. Your home group is the one you take extra interest and become active in.

---

[3]Note: Dr. Bob, one of the founders of AA, said: "There's the hard way and the easy way to stay sober. The hard way is just going to meetings. The easy way is by working with somebody sicker than you (too)." Don't think that because you're new to recovery you can't help another. A person with three weeks of sobriety certainly has a lot of information to give another with only three days.

Group Service

"Becoming active" may be anything from volunteering to make coffee and wash ashtrays to attending business meetings and voting on decisions about the group's structure. Or, it might just involve spending a little time helping another who is suffering from the same fears and loneliness that you knew. Reaching out and helping others combats our selfishness and self-centeredness, and makes us feel great, too. Just helping with the coffee is a good starter for getting active with your home group.

Eventually, consider service work with your home group. This means accepting secretary, treasurer, group service representative, or other service positions. It's fun and very rewarding. It's another level of fulfillment in recovery, where divine order takes over and motivates those who try it.

90 MEETINGS IN 90 DAYS

Making at least one meeting a day is essential during the first three months of recovery. More than one meeting a day, when possible, brings us even closer to the solutions we're seeking.

Yeah, but . . .

If your first thought was *"Yeah, but . . ."* to this suggestion, you're right where you should be. *"Yeah, but . . ."* and *"If only I'd have . . ."* are expressions we addicts use to rationalize and justify our stubbornness. The most overriding characteristic of a drug addict is defiance. The exact definition of defiance is "*a bold resistance to authority*," but very simply, it means rebelliousness and stubbornness. Our stubborn and defiant nature has been part of us for years, and probably won't be leaving very quickly.

Whatever has appeared normal for other people has always seemed foreign to me. I've always been a mutineer. I was the "rebel without a cause" because, "*I don't want to do it if it's right!*" Sometimes I feel as though I was defiant and stubborn even in my mother's womb! That may sound weird, I know, but I think it was true. Probably when it was time to sleep I'd kick and bounce and make all kinds of commotion. I wouldn't be a bit surprised if, instead of gently floating around in the womb and then pushing out with my head first, like most babies, I had tried to kick my way out, or do cartwheels instead!

Don't allow your rebellious attitudes to take the wheel and steer you back to drugs. These 90 meetings in 90 days are important. "*Yeah, but I've got to . ..*" See? Don't "yeah, but . . ." yourself. The opposite of defiance is reliance. "*Don't Defy. Rely!*" That means relying on the meetings, relying on a sponsor, relying on the Twelve Steps and a healthy spiritual direction.

6 . . .

How to

Avoid a Relapse . . .

A relapse is also called a "SLIP," which can stand for Sobriety Lost In Priorities. There are seven different ways sobriety begins to take a back seat to other priorities. These are explained in this chapter.

Relapses seem to occur more often during these periods: the first five to seven weeks of recovery, the fifth through seventh month of recovery, the eleventh month, and the thirteenth month. Use these recovery suggestions to avoid a relapse—especially during these vulnerable periods.

DON'T MISS MEETINGS

Many relapses occur when things are going extremely well. When things are going well it is easy to begin thinking, *"Maybe I don't need these Twelve-Step meetings any more."* This is an attitude of complacency. When you're feeling good, you need a meeting just as much as when you're feeling down. Complacency is always a good topic to discuss at a meeting.

One good friend of mine in early recovery got tripped up by feeling so good, and relapsed. This person called me the next day and described the feeling of being tied to railroad tracks: on one side was the recovery meetings with the winners, and on the other side were the bars and drug houses. My friend said, through much pain and shame, *"I just don't feel like I belong on either side. I'm tied to these tracks, and I feel like I'm going to be crushed, very soon."*

I listened, shocked. Remembering the importance of not calling on a relapsed addict alone, I said I'd call right back, and hung up, trying to find another group member to go with me. Quickly checking with my own sponsor first, the two of us visited my friend at home, wiped away the shame, and went to an afternoon meeting together. My friend is now helping others.

Missing meetings doesn't apply to those who try a couple of Twelve-Step meetings and don't return. That type of person fits the description of *"some are sicker than others*," someone who is not yet willing to go to any length to stay drug-free. What we're concerned with here happens possibly six weeks or six months, or even six years after you start the program. It's as though you begin to feel so good in recovery that you start thinking that meetings aren't important anymore and, crazier yet, start believing it. This complacency, or "*smug satisfaction*," just doesn't happen overnight. A recovering person gradually becomes complacent. He or she may skip a meeting one week, only to develop an attitude the next week of, "*Well, last week I skipped a meeting and I didn't use drugs, so I'll skip again. Besides, I feel good.*"

PRAY REGULARLY

Nearly everyone in recovery occasionally forgets to pray to a Higher Power. Don't get down on yourself if this happens. Just pray later in the day, or the following day, when you remember. A simple habit of praying to one's Higher Power, saying "*Please . . .*" in the morning and "*Thank you . . .*" at night, has brought lasting sobriety and clean-time to millions of addictive people.

A View of Spirituality

The Twelve Steps of recovery are not religious, they are spiritual. Some believe religion saves your soul and prepares you for dying. The Twelve Steps of recovery will save your life and restore your dignity, spirit, and general enthusiasm through "helping others." This spiritual way of life is accented by *"One Day at a Time."*

Many religions have rules to be followed, some so strict that they prohibit caffeine or smoking (which would have cast me into the depths of hell by age twelve!). It is certainly not the purpose of this book to downgrade religion. But spiritual avenues are not the same as religious doctrines. And almost everybody in recovery, with the Twelve Steps as their guidelines, finds a different view of a Higher Power than they had believed in before, whatever church they'd grown up in. I've even known priests who have found a different concept of God through fulfilling the Twelve Steps. Sometime in recovery (and the earlier the better), you will need to come to the realization that God is God, and you are you. You are not God. Merely grasping that realization is making fantastic progress, a giant step forward.

The word "spirituous," which means "containing alcohol," is strangely similar to the word "spiritual." Both will alter the mind if enough is absorbed. The big difference is that the power of alcohol is temporary but destructive. Spirituality is a power, too, positive and permanent once achieved. Remember that spiritual is "full of life, full of love, full of energy."

A few recovering addicts may need to use the slogan *"Act as if . . ."* to overcome their defiant attitudes that nothing is more powerful than "self." But realize that *"self will run riot"* is a major part of the addiction problem. *"Fake it till you make it"* is an expression that has been known to help many an agnostic. Some have lost their lives in relapse because of their close-mindedness. An open mind, as explained earlier, is an important key to sobriety.

Getting into the habit of praying may come slowly. And a spiritual awakening, for most people, takes a long time, although a few may experience it immediately. If believing in a Higher Power is a problem for you today, just quit doubting for a while and use the group as your source of spirituality. Most believe that God talks through others at these meetings.

HAVE ENOUGH CONTACT WITH YOUR SPONSOR

There are times when being out-of-touch with your sponsor can't be helped; for example, when he or she goes on vacation or a business trip, or is temporarily sick. When daily contact with your sponsor is interrupted, for whatever reason, extra effort must be given to reconnecting this communication system. The alternate sponsorship described previously will prevent this breakdown. Daily contact merely shifts over to the alternate, keeping the necessary hook-up fastened tight.

Maintaining contact with your sponsor is most important for achieving quality sobriety, a sobriety with a good emotional feeling. So, if your "little boy" or "little girl" feelings get hurt every so often from your sponsor's directions and guidance, it is merely part of a growing up process in recovery. Your littlechild syndrome is what your sponsor is trying to help you release. Just get back up, wash off the baby bruises and begin calling your sponsor again. It's all part of the healing process of recovery, and everyone walks through it. In short, you probably won't agree with everything your sponsor says. It will take time to change a defiant personality to a responsible, mature, and reliant one. But eventually, it will happen.

Humor and Self-Pity

Poor me . . .
Poor me . . .
Pour me a drink!

Laughter has healing power over many obstacles in recovery—especially self-pity. Sponsors help newcomers overcome self-pity, too. This is an excellent topic for meetings because it seems we all get stuck on the pity-pot at times. Talking about self-pity is one remedy for getting rid of it.

When you were a child, did you ever stand in front of the mirror and laugh at your own facial expressions? Go ahead, do it! We all take recovery very seriously, but remember, it is not a punishment. The punishment of drug addiction is over. We need to lubricate our rusty sense of humor. *"Don't be so serious."* As one North Carolina member said: *"If you're not laughing in your sobriety, you're not taking sobriety seriously enough."* And of course the shorter version of the Serenity Prayer is: *"Lighten up."*

When I was told to find something to laugh at, daily, in this "One day at a time" program of recovery, I thought about it for a while and couldn't come up with any ideas at all. I'd been out of practice a long time. Not being much of a reader at that point, I decided maybe I'd find a joke book at the bookstore, and went shopping for one. Well, there were several of them, so I bought two. It might sound wacky, but for the next few months, every morning for about five minutes I'd read a few of those jokes to myself and go into hysterics. Even today, years later, I don't miss reading the comic section of the daily newspaper.

ADMIT POWERLESSNESS

Step One—the admission that addiction has made one's life completely unmanageable—is the only one of the Twelve Steps that must be taken to perfection. We in recovery find it necessary to review this step daily, and remember the pain it took to find a drug-free lifestyle; to remember our powerlessness and life's unmanageability so that we don't ever return to drugs.

Plain old self-deceit plays a big part in these so-called "slips." A few newcomers go running for the booze (usually wine or beer) upon declaring their powerlessness and unmanageability regarding drugs —as if alcohol weren't a drug. Admitting and accepting one's powerlessness over drugs includes *all* mind-altering chemicals. Don't be a loser by stubbornly experimenting in your recovery program. Your gut feelings tell you that all the mind and body buzzes are out, and will only bring more pain. Put off the booze, too—"*One Day at a Time.*"

BE CAREFUL USING MEDICATIONS

It is not the intent of this book to advise which medications to avoid. It is necessary to note, though, that many physicians are not fully educated on drug addiction and alcoholism. Any doctor in recovery will attest to this. Some medical schools spend very little time on educating their students about addiction. Strange as it may seem in a time of so many problems with booze and drugs, it is true. How does this affect a newcomer in recovery? Drug addicts don't use drugs successfully! Some physicians will prescribe potentially mind-altering medications to recovering people and in so doing, threaten their sobriety.

Cross-Checking Medications

Many recovering addicts have found a way to get through this medication dilemma safely, by cross-checking a prescription before having it filled. This requires some discipline, as you may be physically ill during this process and the relief that the medication can bring is foremost in your mind. If necessary, have another person do the follow-up suggested below. Getting a second opinion on questionable medications can be crucial. Recovering addicts have suffered relapses from not taking the time to cross-reference their prescriptions; others have simply not known why or how to do it.

One reliable source for cross-checking medications is a registered nurse at a detox or treatment center. Nurses in this position are more likely to be aware of which drugs are safe for addicts and which ones need to be avoided. Another good source is your druggist. A smaller pharmacy is best since there's less likely to be a long line of people, and the pharmacist will have more time to spend with you. In either case, simply say that you are an addict in recovery and would like to get a second opinion on the relative safety of the medication that has been prescribed for you. Often, a pharmacist will say, "No, you can't take this, but you can take this other one instead; I'll call the doctor for you and have it changed over."

Recovering drug addicts find extra assurance in telling their doctors and dentists that they're in recovery. Don't feel embarrassed about revealing this. Most physicians probably wish their other patients with destructive addictions would take the same courageous step. Don't be surprised later if either the doctor, dentist, or even pharmacist asks you for advice regarding a patient, patron, or associate of theirs suffering from alcoholism or drug addiction. Both Alcoholics Anonymous and Narcotics Anonymous have great credentials world-wide, and the smarter health professionals realize this.

Over-the-Counter Medications

If you come down with a cold or the flu, instead of purchasing just any cough syrup on the store shelf, buy one that specifies "nonalcoholic" on the label. Avoid brands marked "non-narcotic"—these can be loaded with alcohol. This is very important. When attending Twelve-Step meetings, you'll often hear accounts of how relapses were caused by taking cough medications containing alcohol. Many A.A. and N.A. members suggest avoiding even cold tablets.

One evening, while attending an AA meeting out of town, I noticed the leader giving away red, white, and blue poker chips to the beginners saying, "If anyone would like to join our way of life, we'll give you a white poker chip to keep with your pocket change, to remind you of how you're gambling with your life by drinking." The leader went on to explain that a red chip is taken for three months of sobriety, a blue one for six months, and an annual medallion with a Roman numeral on the front for every year sober.

The leader asked, "Would anyone like to take a white chip and join our way of life?" Well, three people walked up to the front of the room and took their white chips; one asked to explain to the group why he had done so.

"I know this may surprise a few of you," he said, "but I have to keep this thing honest for me." He'd obviously been to the meetings before. "I had a real bad cold last week, and although I'd heard that I should avoid cough medicine containing alcohol, I bought a bottle of (a popular brand) and within two hours after starting with a teaspoon, I was gulping down the whole bottle. Then I went back to the pharmacy and bought three more bottles. My mind tasted the booze in it, and wanted more. So, I thought I'd take a white chip tonight and start again."

The room applauded his honesty. I was highly impressed!

Hospitalizations

If you undergo a hospitalization where strong medications are given, for example in surgery, consider staying in the hospital an extra day or two to take advantage of the controlled environment. When you are discharged, you should be taking nothing stronger than aspirin or Tylenol for pain relief. Remember: "*Drug addicts don't use drugs successfully.*" Keep your sponsor informed about anything having to do with medications that may be happening in your life.

DON'T HOLD GRUDGES OR RESENTMENTS

The number one offender and threat to an addict's recovery is a resentment, or "holding a grudge." This is a luxury that we, as addicts, cannot afford. Anger is poison for us, and a resentment is anger turned inward. Sometimes it's almost as though we nurse an anger or rehearse a grudge until it becomes part of us, until we become sick from the internal turmoil, festering and smoldering away.

The word "resentment" means "to refeel," to feel something bad from the past over again. We all know how painful feelings of resentment are because we are good at rehearsing this character defect. It is another defect of our character grounded in fear and rooted in selfishness. It takes time to understand this. Meanwhile, just try to let it go. Now that you want to change your life, let go of any hatred you feel before it builds up. How important is a grudge, a resentment? Is it important enough to risk a relapse?

Everyone knows that knowledge is powerful, but few know that forgiveness is wealth within. *"Let go and let God."* If you can't discard the grudge, then give it to God. We remind each other at meetings that, *"I can't . . . He can . . . I think I'll just let Him."* Turn your grudge over to your Higher Power. It works very well that way.

One way to guarantee that you will have the last word in a dispute is to apologize. This sounds odd, but it works. Give the other person the right to be wrong, and in so doing, you give yourself the same right (read that one again). Recovery principles teach us that we don't have to be perfect any more, and when we are wrong, to promptly admit it.

If your resentment doesn't leave immediately, pray every day for two weeks to be freed of your resentment. It will leave! This is another excellent topic for discussion at meetings. Overall, remember: *"I can change myself, but I cannot change others."*

There have been so many resentments in my life. The longest one I have ever held onto was probably against my fifth grade teacher; that left almost as soon as I began to pray for the relief from holding that internal anger so long. The most recent resentment I've held was for a next-door neighbor, and even after two solid weeks of praying, this neighbor is still not one of my favorite people! But the difference is, this person doesn't live in my mind; my mind isn't occupied with anger anymore.

USE THE H.A.L.T. FORMULA

Twelve-Step recovery is a simple program for complicated people—meaning us. We tend to complicate some of the ideas that have worked for others because they seem just too simple for us. Don't complicate your recovery. *There may be some people too smart for Twelve Step recovery, but none too dumb.*

Don't Get Hungry

The first letter of H.A.L.T. reminds us not to let ourselves get hungry. When we're hungry, we feel empty, a dangerous feeling for a recovering addict. Begin to eat breakfast. Even a quick scrambled egg or a bowl of cereal will help get you moving, both mentally and physically. A glass of juice is good, too. For many addicts in recovery, breakfast is a neglected meal—and yet it is essential for getting your day off to a good start.

Avoid crash diets in early recovery. Remember: *"First things first."* Your body doesn't need any more shocks at this time. There's plenty of time to become body beautiful. Keep your priorities in order!

Don't Get Angry

The letter "A" in the H.A.L.T. formula is for "*Don't get angry.*" Start talking with your sponsor daily about even the little problems that bother you. Don't let them build. Maybe you got stuck in traffic on the way to work, or maybe the alarm clock didn't go off on time. Maybe the car won't start properly, or the subway is too crowded; all these little things can add up. The build-up of these seemingly minor problems often is more oppressing and difficult to deal with than bigger problems. Why? Because they're often overlooked, or discounted as being too trivial to talk about. Remember, when a burden is shared, it is also halved and cleared. Don't hold them in.

Stop suppressing the little things, but don't unload them on just anyone who will listen. Unload them on your sponsor. That's one of the things that sponsorship is for. Your sponsor knows how to help with the burdens of the day and how to develop a different outlook on problems.

Another solution to anger is to exhaust yourself with exercise. Something that appears overwhelming right now can seem trivial after a good physical workout.

The Serenity Prayer has helped many people deal with sudden bursts of anger. Try saying this prayer ten times when you get angry and experience its power.

God grant me the Serenity
to accept the things I cannot change,
the Courage to change the things I can,
and the Wisdom to know the difference.

Don't Get Lonely

Recovering addicts tend to be a lonely breed and need to reach out to others. Not surprisingly, other addicts are about the only people who understand our bouts of loneliness and how to avoid them. *"Go to meetings early, and leave late"* is good advice, but take it further. Begin to reach out to others in recovery. Today or tomorrow, try the following idea and see if you don't feel better immediately.

When you arrive at a Twelve-Step meeting, shake everyone's hand and say, "Hi, my name is . . .. How're you doing?" You'll notice how much better you feel, but more important, you'll sense you belong there—and you do! If you can't do this yet, try it later this week or next week. Eventually, you'll be looking the other person directly in the eyes and feeling great about yourself.

Another idea for filling the void of loneliness is what some call "telephone therapy." This is simply calling another person in recovery to say "Hi . . .." Asking others at the meetings for their telephone numbers is very normal, and one rarely asks why. Before long, any newcomer has fifteen to twenty telephone numbers of people who really care, and will reach out to help one another. Try calling someone

just to say "Hello." It gives that person a warm
feeling, too.

Don't Get Tired

The last letter in the formula is "T" for *"Don't Get
Tired."* Getting a restful night of sleep is essential to
recovery. If you have trouble falling asleep at night,
switch to decaffeinated coffee in the evening, and
remember that most sodas are loaded with caffeine
and sugar. Try diet decaffeinated sodas, especially in
the evening. You'll notice how much more restful
your sleep will be. Try a short nap in the afternoon.
"Easy Does It," yes, but do it.

7 . . .

Making Friends
With Time . . .

This chapter addresses a question many new-comers to recovery ask. "What am I going to do with all this free time?"

My whole drug-induced lifestyle revolved around my obsession with the drug. To help you understand what this is like, try to remember the first love of your life. Can you remember how much that little boy or girl consumed all of your thoughts and energies? Now multiply that obsession by a thousand or more, and it still won't come even close. Driving to get the drug; the haggling about how to get it cheaper; the conniving and deceitful conversations and actions—then once it's consumed, the process starts all over again. Before the effects had even begun to wear off, I'd be running out for more, and more, and more.

The tightly-wound clock in the twenty-four hours of drug addiction never stopped ticking. It was as though an alarm was going to go off any minute, but not just to wake me up in the morning—it would go off like one hell of an internal bomb, which only strung-out addicts have experienced.

You know, if a person is used to driving a car with a clutch for several years, and then suddenly finds himself behind the wheel of an automatic, chances are the left leg will want to do something in place of pushing the clutch in. It may even try to ride the brake! Early recovery will feel like there are many left feet with nothing to do, and if they are not kept busy, they will get bored, or go where they don't belong.

In early recovery, it may seem as if there is too much extra time. But six months from now, you'll probably wish you could find an extra hour or two in the day. At first, however, this additional time may seem a little scary. The drugs you've taken have probably repressed and muffled your skills and talents. Being afraid of doing something new, or even something you once liked, leaves you paralyzed, a feeling disguised as boredom. Boredom can lead to feelings of self-pity and the attitude that nothing is okay or working out in your recovery. If you start to have these thoughts or feelings, remember that the letters in the word FEAR stand for "*False Emotion Appearing Real*." Boredom is only a false emotion—a false message resulting from a fear of the new direction we need to take in our daily lives.

CONCENTRATE ON THE PRESENT

Newcomers often have one eye on yesterday, and the other on tomorrow—which tends to make you cross-eyed. Try to keep your thinking in the now. Time is on our side. To illustrate how time can be your friend, ask yourself if you are, at this very instant, in extreme physical pain? Can you remember a time when you were feeling a lot worse off, when the pain was constant? Then, you'd have given anything to trade places with yourself today . . . right? In recovery, you'll slowly come to terms with "Mr. Time," and realize that he's not your enemy. He's your friend.

NEW HOBBIES AND RENEWED SKILLS

While some of us in sobriety will rediscover former pleasures, many will have to be open-minded enough to develop new interests. As you begin to survey the many options available to you, be aware of a pleasant feeling of inner energy starting to flow, or a feeling of aliveness, inspiring good thoughts. Just how do we go about getting in touch with this new flow of energy and thinking, to produce new action? How do we occupy those left feet? Well, we can begin by going to a local bookstore or library and scanning the section on hobbies and interests. Thumb through some of the books and see if the activities appeal to your present interests.

Just be on guard for that familiar old mind-tape that might try to divert you by saying things like,

"You know you can't do this, because you're too stupid." or "You're not good enough—who do you think you're fooling?" These are self-imposed lies, and you know it. Sometimes, it's easy to forget that we don't have to be perfect anymore; that just because we may not be able to do something the best, fastest, or biggest, doesn't mean we can't enjoy pursuing it for our own creative pleasure. We don't have to compete in hobbies and crafts. We may never paint like Pablo Picasso, or play the guitar like Eric Clapton, but we sure can relax and have a good time. In recovery, we begin to realize that joy comes from the everyday actions and the daily journey, not from the end results.

Begin to consciously plan some activities. Buy a few books, or just make a list of the things that spark your enthusiasm. Then set some goals which further explore some of these things. Ask yourself where you can get more information or supplies to begin this fun process. Find out if you're going to need specific training and where you can find people to teach you. Narrow your list; be as specific as possible about pursuing certain talents. Reread your list daily and begin to imagine yourself doing some of these things.

Cultivate the attitude of "I can . . ." rather than the old one of "I can't . . ." as you visualize yourself in the process of doing your new fun activity. Surround yourself with positive affirmations, giving yourself positive energies and good thoughts. Remember that all of our thoughts can generate powerful energy and actions, so review your thinking regularly. Stay directed and focused on what it is you want to pursue and what you want the experience to feel and be like.

Above all, remember that you may not enjoy everything new that you try, or the old things that you rediscover. That's okay. There are plenty of exciting and challenging things in this world just waiting to be found out about—just waiting for that left foot to get active with!

Maybe a crossword puzzle in the daily newspaper suits your fancy; or jigsaw puzzles. Gardening can seem like hard work for one person, and a relaxing, God-sent hobby for another. Try to identify you own unique strengths and interests. We all have different interests and abilities. The best advice is to try out a variety of hobbies and activities to see if any of them are right for you before taking a big plunge and spending a lot of money. Don't buy an expensive set of golf clubs before you've tried golfing. Shoot a few buckets of balls on a driving range first. Test the waters. If it feels comfortable, go on in.

Be sure you choose something that you can do daily. One can't go fishing every day of the year, but one can make flies and lures during bad weather days. Get the picture? Sewing, auto maintenance, garment weaving, gourmet cooking, metal shop, learning a new language or brushing up on an old one—the list can go on and on, but now you add to it, or draw from it.

Music

Many people go through life saying things like, "If only I'd taken piano lessons when I was young . . ." or, "I wish I'd kept up with the saxophone . . .." So, why not now? No, not to become a concert pianist or a professional performer. We're talking about a hobby. What about guitar, flute, drums, violin, trumpet, organ, or tuba? What about singing lessons? There are many choral groups looking for new voices.

If learning to play a musical instrument interests you at all, consider renting the instrument from a music store to get started. Most music stores will apply the rental toward a later purchase. But take a month or so to see if you enjoy the instrument before investing much money. Remember that recovering addicts have a tendency to be impulsive, to do something extreme without thinking it through first. Most stores that rent musical instruments give lessons, too. It might be best to tell the shop owner up front what you're trying to do. Explain that one lesson every two weeks, or only a half-hour lesson per week, will be more suitable for you (*"Easy Does It"*). Remember—hobby, not super-stardom!

Art

If music doesn't interest you, there are many other areas to explore. What about number paintings? Try mixing some paints and creating your own shades. What about sculpting with clay, wood, or stone? Call up an art store and tell them that you want to do it just for fun, and ask how you can get started. If they suggest signing up for a sculpting course being offered in a few months, say, "Okay, but can you give me a few supplies now to start chipping or whittling away with?"

Other Ideas

Let your mind wander as you consider other possible hobbies. Possibilities include building: model airplanes, boats, or cars. Be sure to have plenty of ventilation in the room when applying glue—but you've probably already thought of that!

Other pastimes that you can't practice daily, but which would give you good exercise and a good time are bowling, basketball, tennis, or golf. Want to be different? What about archery? Sporting goods stores have whatever you need to get started and they can direct you to help or lessons or to others who are interested in the same sport. When you try one of these activities, if you don't enjoy it, don't do it again. You don't have to please anyone but yourself.

Some in recovery love a good softball game, and many areas even have teams made up of recovering addicts. Just show up with a glove. Notice how the other players in recovery drop balls, too. It's only for fun, and it provides another way to help you learn to laugh at yourself, and laugh with others.

RECOVERY GAMES

Your social skills—getting along with others, overcoming shyness, or learning how not to be a loner anymore—will slowly improve as your recovery progresses. Playing a board game is one way to create an atmosphere of socializing, yet it also gives everyone an activity to focus on—an activity that has to do with what you are learning about as well as what you already know.

Consider playing the game of *"Yeah, but . . .."* This is an addiction trivia game with both alcohol- and drug-related trivia cards. Another excellent board game is the humorous *"Addictionary 'You know . . ..'"* These games are available at many Twelve-Step gift shops or bookstores, or directly through The Institute of Substance Abuse Research.[4] Both games are perfect for socializing with others and are loads of fun. Remember, friend, the pain of drug addiction is over ("One Day at a Time") and recovery is very enjoyable.

"What am I going to do with all this extra time?" Before too long, you'll be saying, "What extra time?"

---

[4]I.S.A.R., P.O. Box 6837, Vero Beach, FL 32961-3121

8 . . .

You Are
What You Eat . . .

One vital area of recovery that is too often overlooked is learning to eat wholesome and healthy foods. Improper food planning, such as selecting too much of one type of food and avoiding another altogether, can unknowingly invite a relapse.

Good nutrition alone will not "cure" alcoholism and drug addiction. The roots of any addiction are too deeply twisted in the social, personal, and spiritual soil of the person for just one thing to solve it. But there is no doubt that good nutrition can create a peaceful place for the mind to be, a place where sobriety is easier to imagine, to seek, and to obtain.

One of the last subjects a newly recovering drug addict might want to read about is eating healthy food. But before closing your mind to this subject, ask yourself one question: would you hit and hurt your best friend? No, of course not. Well, since part of recovery is about making friends with ourselves, and, yes, eventually becoming best friends with ourselves, we need to stop hurting ourselves by eating the wrong foods. Good nutrition is basic to a drug-free life.

The human body is a chemical mixture containing 100 billion cells, which need nutrition for building blocks. Drugs, alcohol, and food change the body's chemistry. The direction of change—good or bad—is what we'll look at here.

An amazing experiment was conducted with two groups of rats: one group received good, nutritious foods, and the second group received food with very poor nutritional content. Both groups of rats were given the choice of either plain water or an alcohol and water mixture to drink. Oddly enough, the second group (the ones receiving poor nutrition) began drinking the alcohol mixture. The first group of rats, the ones receiving good nutrition, didn't touch any of the alcohol/water mixture.

Later, the diet of the second group was gradually improved, and as it did, the rats began to drink less and less of the alcoholic water, and more plain water. This experiment says an awful lot about how important good nutrition is to recovery!

Addicts have a long history of horrible eating habits. When we start to feel a little low, our poor nutrition makes us feel even worse. If we feel bad enough, we reach for booze or some other drug. In early recovery, we addicts are used to the sudden shifts in blood sugar from active drug addiction. Booze and other drugs raise blood sugar so quickly that we're used to that "quick fix" feeling; we even seek out stressful situations—which also raise blood sugar levels—in early recovery in order to get the same feelings. We drive too fast, walk too fast, drink too much coffee, eat lots of sugar, and start arguments over unimportant things.

So, we addicts need to be careful to avoid coffeholism and chocaholism as we become stressed-out sweetaholics! WARNING! Excessive caffeine and sweets (simple carbohydrates) increase the chances of relapsing with drinking and drugs because of the effect on blood glucose levels.

I have not designed this short chapter to promote any kind of special diet. Instead, I will outline a simple plan of four essential food categories that should be eaten daily by the recovering addict. Now let's take a look at the different groups of foods, and start eating balanced meals so you'll feel good.

CONSTRUCTIVE CARBOHYDRATES

Carbohydrates are your body's main energy source.
Have some healthy carbohydrates at every meal!

Fresh Fruit
Fresh Vegetables
Whole Grains

FUNDAMENTAL FATTY ACIDS

Safflower Oil
Wheat Germ Oil
Olive Oil
Cod Liver Oil

Have a little every day. Butter and margarine are
not essential fats; eat IN MODERATION.

PRIMARY PROTEIN

Eggs
Milk
Cheese
Yogurt
Fish
Fowl (chicken, turkey, etc.)
Red Meat

Protein is the essential building block for your
body. Have some protein at every meal. Nuts and

seeds are also good secondary sources for both protein and carbohydrates.

VITAL VITAMINS & MANDATORY MINERALS

Because you probably haven't eaten well in a long time, you need to replenish these important nutrients. Look for a good complete multiple vitamin with added minerals—calcium, magnesium, potassium, zinc, and iron are the most important. Remember, you get what you pay for. Some vitamins are very cheap and will not be absorbed as well by your body. If you are in doubt, ask your pharmacist to recommend a particular brand. Always consult your physician for specific guidance about taking supplements.

THE TRUTH ABOUT JUNK FOOD

Avoid the junk foods, and you will avoid feeling like junk. The following foods are not good for you; go easy on them, or avoid them altogether if you can:

Sugar
White Flour
Salt
Coffee, Tea, Colas (caffeine)
Sweetened fruit drinks
Candy
Ice Cream
Cakes, Cookies, Pies, etc. made with white flour
Foods with preservatives, artificial coloring, and other chemicals

Try to avoid eating "fast food" constantly. These meals are not balanced and it isn't good to be in the habit of eating "on the run." Food will always taste better and be more nutritious if prepared with care and eaten in a relaxed environment.

Some schools of thought about recovery from drug addiction suggest that it is best to immediately quit using sugar and caffeine. People are divided on this question, so you'll need to decide what seems best for you. But at least consider switching to decaffeinated coffee or tea after the first morning cup, and try decaffeinated sodas, too. Try substituting fruit for candy and other sweets.

For more about healthy eating, read the book *Eating Right To Live Sober*, by Katherine Ketcham and L. Ann Mueller, M.D. and look through your library's books on nutrition for additional general information.

Note: Don't try to quit smoking or diet to lose or gain weight during the first six months of your recovery. Many people feel even a year is better, though there are of course some who believe in changing everything immediately. In researching for this book, we have discovered that following the slogan "First things first" works best. It just makes sense to handle one body shock at a time.

9 . . .

No Need

To Be Tense . . .

Learning how to relax, physically and mentally, is a precious ability for the recovering addict, whose tension levels are bound to be high.

Physical relaxation in recovery is sometimes overlooked because the emotional and spiritual repairs that are so desperately needed are given priority. But physical relaxation is so important it should be put near the top of the list. The tension that drug addiction brings about follows us into recovery. Yes, you hear people say at meetings, *"Easy does it!"* But you may wonder how to follow that advice. Here is a remarkably effective breathing and relaxation exercise for reducing stress.

Sit comfortably in a straight-backed chair, resting your head either against the top of the chair or the wall behind it. Sit up straight with your legs comfortably positioned in front of you and hands in your lap. If possible, remove your shoes and loosen any tight clothing. Be sure that you are in a quiet place. A sound-effects tape with soft, soothing sounds such as a forest with birds and breezes, or ocean waves on a beach with sea gulls, will help.

Since this exercise should be done with your eyes closed, read the following instructions a few times to get the idea of the sequence, or have someone read them aloud to you while you are doing the exercises.

1. Tighten the muscles in your feet and the calves of your legs and breath in and out slowly and deeply three times. Now relax those muscles.

2. Tighten the muscles in your knees and thighs and breathe in and out slowly and deeply three times. Now relax completely.

3. Tighten the muscles in your lower back and buttocks and breathe in and out three times. Now relax for a moment, breathing normally.

4. Tighten the muscles in your stomach area and breathe in and out three times (through your chest). Again, relax.

5. Tighten the muscles in your upper back and chest, and breathe in and out three times. Relax.

6. Tighten the muscles in your shoulders, arms, and hands, breathing in and out three times. Then, relax.

7. Tighten the muscles in your neck and jaw, including your tongue, breathing in and out three times. Relax for a moment. Tighten the muscles in your face and head, including your cheeks, nose, and around your eyes, breathing in and out three times. Now, relax and feel the slight tingling of your body releasing itself from tension and anxiety.

8. Using both hands, massage your temples—the area next to your eyes. Then slowly massage your forehead, moving down to your upper cheekbones and around your eyes and nose. Then massage the area above your ears, around the back of your ears, and then circle down onto your neck and shoulders. (The entire massage should take about 30 seconds, though some sore areas may take a little extra massaging.)

9. Now rest your hands in your lap again and take three deep breaths. Keeping your eyes closed, begin to picture a very comfortable place, such as a forest, a mountain, or a beach setting; choose a place that feels tranquil or peaceful for your mind to drift to. After resting for five minutes or so, you've completed the exercise.

It may take a few practice sessions before you begin to experience the imagery—the quiet, comfortable place—in its full setting, but each time it will be clearer and closer.

Throughout the day you can practice parts of this exercise, even when other people are around. For example, just massaging your forehead briefly can take you back to that comfortable setting. Also, at any time of day, you can tighten a few muscles, breathe deeply, and relax them.

Anything that makes us feel great, we tend to try to sell to others. Keep this exercise secret. Don't tell everyone you meet how to relax. Some may take it as an insult. People will begin to notice your increased calmness anyway, as you continue to practice the technique regularly. Eventually, if you think someone is sincere and teachable, then share this chapter, but don't try to push it onto others. *"Live and let live."*

Be sure to check with your physician in case there might be a medical reason that you should avoid doing this exercise. If for some reason you are unable to do it, try just listening to relaxation tapes; they're very popular today. These tapes can be found in thrift shops, bookstores and many libraries. Begin to learn how to relax, and practice it daily. You'll think more clearly and enjoy your day much more. *EASY DOES IT!*

10 . . .

Necessary
Attitudes . . .

How we handle everyday problems affects our sobriety. This chapter explains how to keep problems from upsetting us and identifies some of the other mature qualities which strengthen our sobriety.

By now, you're probably beginning to realize that the real hornets' nest is not the drug itself. Addicted lives are muddled; usually every area of life is confused. In the past, we've used drugs to avoid this self-induced hornets' nest of problems, and have been badly stung in the process. Now we know there isn't any chemical answer to our problems. The real problem is inside us and that's where we must look to change. In fact, our entire attitude and outlook on life will need a complete overhaul. To paraphrase one Twelve-Step book: *An entire psychic*

*change needs to take place, or there is very little hope
of recovery.*

WHY WON'T MY PROBLEMS GO AWAY?

How do I deal with my everyday minor problems?
How should I react to life's unavoidable turmoil?
When will the worrisome moments disappear?

Everyone in recovery slowly realizes that problems
don't go away just because we're not using drugs
anymore. We also slowly realize that it's how we
handle our inevitable problems that is the gauge for
how much wisdom we're accumulating, *"One day at a
time."*

We all have problems; we can't avoid them. Small
ones, medium ones, and big ones. Problems are a part
of life. Problems should not be thought of as things
that interfere with being content and happy. They
don't—unless we force them to. That's right! Only
when we *force* problems to interfere with our contentment are they able to do that very thing.

When two people face the same problem at the
same time, two very different responses can occur.
One person forces the problem upon himself. Frust-
rated because there is no immediate solution, he becomes discontented and unhappy. This person lacks
an understanding of himself and life. The other
person, facing the same problem, refuses to force the
problem onto himself. This second person allows
himself some room for contentment; or we could say

that he doesn't subscribe to discontentedness. How does he do this? By fully understanding that life is *supposed* to have problems, and by developing the strength and wisdom to accept them. We all need to be reminded of this fact occasionally.

Problems are a normal part of everyone's life. Finding answers to our problems in recovery is both difficult and important. However, when we realize a solution isn't always found when or where we want it, and when we refuse to feel miserable about it, we have begun to achieve wisdom.

It's very simply stated in the Serenity Prayer: *"God, grant me the serenity to accept the things I cannot change . . ."* Suppose that there's a problem that seems to be preventing you from achieving contentment or "serenity." The prayer goes on: ". . . *the courage to change the things I can . . .* " Is there something you yourself can do to solve the problem? If so, fine! Do it! If not, the next part of the prayer says: ". . . *and the wisdom to know the difference."* The problems you cannot solve now you must accept and live with.

People who try to practice this principle in their lives find that what makes them happy is not having or finding the answer to every problem that comes down the pike. It's how they handle the traffic heading down that avenue that really brings contentment and happiness.

The longer we go to meetings, the greater the difference in how we think, and feel, and live, and yes—in how we handle problems. Wisdom is progressive, and progressive means "advancing step by step."

God, grant me the serenity
To accept the things I cannot change,
The courage to change the things I can,
And the wisdom to know the difference.

It is almost as if you can say to yourself, "Ho-hum, another problem for me to solve (perhaps)? No answers or solutions right now? Okay, I'll just handle it another day. Ho-hum!" It is actually that easy.

DETERMINATION

We need enthusiasm and determination for recovery. When you were young and just learning to ride a bicycle, what was the first thing you did when you fell off? You immediately got back on again. You refused to be defeated. This wonderful childlike attitude of determination needs to be revived now. Place the accent on simply not accepting defeat in your quest for sobriety. You can do this sobriety thing, and you truly know it. You've been up against much harder walls than recovery. This time it will work! *"This time my attitude is strengthened with gratitude. This time it WILL work!"*

MATURE ATTITUDES

"Why don't you grow up?" That statement has followed some of us around constantly in our journey

of life. We'll need to develop some mature attitudes to throw off the childishness that has shaped our thoughts and behaviors. Let's look at some of these changes.

We're not impatient anymore. We accept reasonable delays. "*I am very patient; I am, I am, I am.*" (Say it, then you'll feel it.)

We control our temper, and we do not panic. "*I am very tolerant; I am, I am, I am.*"

Our feelings are not easily hurt anymore. We see the humor in the problems we face and in our reactions to them. "*I now have a great sense of humor.*"

We stop worrying about the things we can't change. "*I now accept all the things I can't change. I am at peace. I am, I am, I am.*"

We stop "showing off," and avoid bragging. "*I am what I am, and that's all that I need to be.*"

We begin to enjoy the good fortunes of others, and feel honestly glad for their successes. We outgrow jealousy and envy toward others. "*I am grateful for who I am and what I have.*"

We stop complaining when we lose; we stop the whining. "*I am a good loser. I am, I am, I am.*"

We avoid self-pity. Only a child sits on the pity-pot. *"I am not dominated by the child within anymore. I am mature. I am, I am, I am."*

We stop the "Yeah, but . . ." expressions, and bypass the excuses and self-deceiving thoughts and actions. *"I am now responsible and dependable. I am, I am, I am."*

We become more open-minded each day, and good listeners, too. *"I am grateful for criticism from others, and I am improving daily. I am maturing, more and more and more. I am, I am, I am."*

Repeat these simple phrases daily and they will become realities. Don't worry if you don't fully understand the benefits of some of these statements just yet. You will! Leave a bookmark here and review these thoughts often, especially as you begin and end each day.

11 . . .

Recovery
"In All Our Affairs" . . .

This chapter discusses how the principles of recovery apply to some common areas of concern such as denial, fears of rejection, judgmental attitudes, and other addictions.

Much like alcoholism, drug addition is a disease that tells us "We don't have a disease." How often have addicts told themselves "I'll quit tomorrow?" For many unfortunates, the tomorrows add up to a permanent six-foot berth below ground. Addiction is a disease of denial. Why else would some people, after repeated D.U.I. convictions, still defiantly say, "I can handle it. I can stop anytime I want to?" How can anyone deny his or her dis-EASE? Simple! He or she has been programmed since the crib to deny so much, denial just comes naturally.

When you see someone you haven't seen for a while and ask, "How're you doing?" you know what he's going to say, "Fine!" His car may be in the shop, he may have been up most of the night worrying about his family, and his dog just died, but—"I'm fine! Everything's fine!"

It would be interesting to observe the reaction if we answered "How're you doing?" with something like this,. "Well, I'm kind of overwhelmed with the fear of calamity, broke, and starting a grieving process." Most people probably would smile and say "Great, great; good seeing you again," and quickly depart.

Some of us learned to deny our true condition and feelings at an early age. We were told, "Big boys don't cry." We began to hold back or deny our emotions. Preventing the tears from flowing is painful, as most of us already know. "Little girls must not get angry," and a child prepares to go through life denying yet another emotion. For some of us, these messages were interpreted as "Don't feel!"

This denial factor, which causes us to misinterpret messages, weaves in and out of our recovery. If we dig deeply enough, we could all find examples of how we've misinterpreted messages. Denial is a big problem in society, and it's not easily overcome. The subliminal message of some beer commercials on T.V., costing millions to produce, is there to coax us into having "just one—besides, you can't have any fun without it." Deep in your heart you know that boozing people aren't as beautiful as those advertisements try to telegraph to our subconscious. They are not as interesting or as attractive as the ads would have us believe and they stink of booze besides. Did you ever see a hangover commercial saying, "Come on, just one more drink before visiting the porcelain throne . . .?"

Shakespeare wrote, "To thine own self be true." Start to erase a few of the old tapes from your childhood that you know don't apply to your life today. It's true; life has given us some pretty big bumps and bruises. But what are you going to do about it now? The scars have begun to disappear, and the sour past will develop into a sweet future by taking all the Twelve Steps of recovery.

The book titled *The Search for Serenity - And How to Achieve It* by Lewis F. Presnall is highly recommended reading. It has helped many people put their lives back together. The chapter "The World of Beginning Again" is what is happening to you. And that process has already started. Just think, *"I never have to depend upon a chemical for my daily existence again!"* You are free—with a purpose in life.

JUDGMENTAL ATTITUDES

My perception of a situation puts me in judgment of that situation, good or bad. My opinions about anything or anyone are the ways I judge the world around me. Even "It's a beautiful day" or "It's a horrible day" are judgments. Often we find ourselves judging the way others dress, or comb their hair, how they eat, or do their work.

Being judgmental toward others, or even too critical of ourselves, isn't being fair to our new-found self in recovery, not to mention to others. To degrade others (even in your thinking) is to cheapen yourself. Everyone has a purpose in God's world, and by now, you're starting to see this. Look at it this way: if we complain about another, or even ourselves, we are complaining about God's handiwork—and implying that we know better than God.

Begin to compliment others instead of complaining, and soon you'll be complimenting yourself without any false pride. Look for the good in others, and you'll start to accent the good in yourself. If, after a while, this judgmental attitude is still dominating your thinking, just write this down on a small piece of paper: "I don't want to judge others and be dominated by negative thinking. I don't want to condemn and criticize myself, either." Then put this piece of paper in your Bible or your recovery textbook. It may make no sense to you now, but just watch how your mind soon clears away the unfavorable pattern of thoughts. Other problems can be worked out this way, too.

COMPLIMENTS

Many people truly do not know how to accept a compliment or affirmation. Have you ever been given a compliment, only to belittle, or reject it? For example, someone says, "That's a good-looking jacket!" and your immediate reply is "Oh, I got it at the discount store" or, "My wife picked it out." The next time a direct compliment is given to you, and many compliments will come your way after you've been drug-free for a while, remember to make direct eye contact and simply say "Thank you!" It's fun being more assertive and letting others know that you're worthy of their compliments. Practice saying "Thank you!" or "Thanks, I appreciate it!" *Keep It Simple.*

BLUSHING

Everyone knows that when people are drugged up their feelings are turned off. They are numbed to all genuine feelings. Some people who don't use drugs bring on this "nonfeeling" effect by suppressing their emotions. Have you ever known people who never blush? It's as if they don't feel. Many people believe that blushing means not being assertive. A few in early recovery go through a confused stage of thinking that blushing isn't good; that a person who blushes is showing weakness. During this normal stage of getting to know who you are—making friends with yourself—begin to realize that blushing is actually a good reaction.

I'm not talking just about reddening of the cheeks, either; when you flush with a childlike smile, you're showing feelings, and that's good! So put this "blushing is bad" message out of your mind and replace it with *"Blushing is a way of showing that 'Yes, I feel."*

FEARS OF REJECTION AND FAILURE

Some people lead miserable lives of failure because they focus so much on trying to please others, rather than themselves (see the next chapter, for advice for "Family Members, Friends, and Employers"). At meetings, a common phrase is *"I come first!"* It makes sense. To quote another common phrase, *"Your life is a divine gift for you to live, not for someone else to live for you."* We need to cherish this gift. *"I am what I am."*

Many nonassertive people are troubled with doubt and indecision. Many go overboard in a frantic popularity contest which turns into constant "people pleasing"—meaning behaviors like saying yes when you want to say no, giving compliments when you don't really mean it, or following along with another when you don't really care to.

This exaggerated fear of rejection is a negative power that will only eat away at you. Consider the following idea: some people will like you and encourage you, and others may criticize and avoid you. Don't get involved in judging people according to how they react to you. Say to yourself (and mean it): *"Your opinion of me is none of my business."* When we are walking the street of spiritual progress, we know we're okay.

PAYING OUR DEBTS

It is best to understand from the beginning that your Higher Power wants you to be happy and contented in sobriety. Discard any "punishing-God" ideas and images you may have had. God wants you to have health, wealth, inner success and exterior order. Don't forget, however, that recovery is a process of gradual growth, not an event. It doesn't happen overnight. Slowly, your recovery program will build a foundation for your wants and needs.

Most drug addicts are in debt at the start of sobriety. Remember, *"Easy Does It"* when paying off the bills. A good suggestion for dealing with this problem is to write out a list of all creditors and the amount owed to each. Then give a copy of the list to your sponsor. Your sponsor will help you to develop a plan for becoming debt-free, and to see the importance of making small but regular payments to people you owe money. A few dollars paid to each creditor, regularly and responsibly, may not completely satisfy them, but they won't refuse the money, either. Stay in tune with your sponsor's guidance in this area. Let your sponsor carry all the fear. He or she knows what to do with it, and will slowly teach you to do the same.

"YEAH, BUT . . ."

"Yeah, but . . ." you've come this far; you've cared enough to read this far. Maybe you've even started on

the road to recovery and tried some of our suggestions. Great! The rest is up to you.

"Yeah, but . . ." you say, "it's not always easy." I
didn't say it would be; nobody ever said it would be
easy. This recovery route is sometimes a rough road.
There may be detours, turn-arounds, full stops. But
there are no dead-ends; you can always start up
again. And you will. No, it won't always be easy, but
you CAN do it.

You can, that is, if you believe you can. So, the
first—and last—thing you must do is convince
yourself. Repeat your recovery beliefs every day, first
thing in the morning and last thing at night.

Read—and read again—books like this that are
designed to help and encourage you. Return to those
pages that you know will help you to build your
image of yourself. Read—and reread—the pages that
make you feel good. Keep track of your progress up
the Recovery Chart (p.15). Keep on; keep on; keep
on. *One day at a time.*

You've found by now that you can't do this
recovery thing alone. I hope you've already reached
out to one or more of the recovery groups. Don't stop
reaching out. When your own recovery feels right,
reach out to help the next addict—out and up.

Keep on improving your own physical well-being.
Rest, exercise, nutrition and hygiene are vital to your
recovery. Establish and be aware of your own routines
for all four. Read other books; attend classes; join

groups; seek help. Make the care and maintenance of your body an important part of your recovery. Remember the energy you used to find to destroy yourself? Use that energy now to rebuild yourself.

There's a lot to learn about spirituality. It may seem simple at first—and it is—but there's more to it. As you recover, search for a greater understanding of your spiritual self. You may make some progress alone; you'll make more progress if you reach out to others.

"Yeah, but . . .." No more "Yeah, buts . . .." You can do it. Look at yourself, you've come this far. Self-examination will help you to see that your recovery is progressing. Take some time each day to look at yourself, your routines, your habits, your attitudes. Help yourself to become what you want to be, one step at a time, "*one day at a time.*"

PART TWO . . .

For Family, Friends and Employers of Recovering Addicts

12 . . .

A Guide to Codependency

. . . for the family, friends and employers of recovering addicts

Addiction is a family disease affecting over seventy million Americans. In this chapter we look at suggestions for overcoming the dysfunctional attitudes and behaviors of codependency, and improving communication skills within the family.

The theme of this chapter is, "*Stop being the antidote for the addict's pain!*" Many friends and family members (including employers and teachers) shield addicts from the consequences of their addiction, hurting them in the long run by postponing the day when they must face up to their problem. It hurts the helper too, locking him or her into a pattern of thinking similar to the addict's, involving denial, resentment, and distortion.

Being the antidote for the addict's pain involves a variety of actions. For example, when an addict is too sick or hung over to go to work, his wife might call work and make excuses, saying perhaps that he has the flu. Then in turn—and this happens frequently as the disease progresses—friends on the job conceal the secret of his alcohol or drug problems by doing enough of the workload so the many absences aren't noticed. Even the supervisor can become involved, especially if he himself drinks or drugs on occasion, as he will be more sympathetic. The addict's rationalizations, pleas and promises are incredibly believable.

People closely involved with addicts are called codependents. These are the addict's family members, friends, coworkers, employers, or teachers. The word codependent can be broken down into its prefix, "co," meaning "together or cooperative" and the root word "dependent," meaning "taking support or aid from another; subject to another's rule." The definition of codependent might be paraphrased as one who conforms to another's rule, or more precisely here, to addiction.

Many people close to addicts will deny having been touched by the disease, saying things like, *"It's his life; I don't care."* At the other extreme, codependents express deep resentments for the behavior of the drug-user. *"If she loved her family, she wouldn't take those drugs."* Both approaches are harmful and reinforce the addict's denial by either minimizing the problem or putting him on the defensive.

When those closely involved with addicts begin to understand addiction and codependency, these misguided statements stop. They learn that drug addicts love their family and friends but they are victims of a disease and an obsession, powerless and out-of-control. Codependents who learn the facts about drug addiction begin to see the drug addict as a sick person whose behavior toward them is an expression of that sickness. If the addict could stop, he or she would do just that. Only a very sick person would inflict such pain and suffering on himself or herself, over and over again.

SYMPTOMS OF CODEPENDENCY

Codependency is a way of living, thinking, and feeling. Often, it is insidious and unrecognized. To find if and how you've been affected by this disorder, answer the following questions honestly.

1. Does much of your mental energy focus on solving the addict's problems or relieving his or her pain?

2. Do you often try to manipulate the addict into doing things your way?

3. Does the reflection of the drug addict's behavior make you feel dirty, too?

4. Does your self-esteem seem to come from easing the torment and suffering that addiction creates?

5. Does the thought of "just giving up" make you feel more safe and secure?

If you've answered "yes" to at least three of these questions, then you are probably a codependent. Read on for what can be done about this.

THE BAD/GOOD SYNDROME

Recovery from addiction is a gradual process requiring patience, love, and understanding from codependents. Helping the addict means putting a stop to believing in the bad/good syndrome, the idea that addicts are bad and that bad should be punished. Would you insist that a mental patient do things your way? No. Yet the sick drug addict often hears, "*Why did you . . .? I'm tired of your . . ..*" The message that this translates into for the drug addict is "*You are a bad person.*" He becomes defensive and even more resistant to change. Twelve-Step recovery for codependents gets this bad/good misconception straightened out quickly. Disease means sick!

To further counteract the "bad/good" syndrome it is also wise to avoid rewarding the addict who begins a recovery program. The need to seek and hold onto recovery for oneself, not for outside rewards, is basic to success. In your own and the addict's best interests, stop using punishment and rewards as a means of controlling him. You cannot force him to recover; you certainly know that by now.

ECHOES FROM CHILDHOOD

Many codependents think and act as they do partly because they were affected by the alcohol or drug abuse of others when they were children. Many began taking on nurturing roles too early, when their parents were unable to act like parents because of drugs or alcoholism. Some codependents grew up influenced by the extreme perfectionism of parents who were not addicts but exhibited the same dysfunctional personality traits—the so-called "dry alcoholics." Everything had to be so perfect while growing up; mistakes were not allowed. Other codependents grew up with varying degrees of neglect.

Whatever confusion these types of upbringings might have caused, it's important to put them to rest, now! These events, no matter how terrifying or embarrassing, are over and done. They are in the past. That part of your life is over, and to relive it is unhealthy; is not reality. Remember, reality is the present. The past must be let go of, once and for all. *"Let go, let God"* is one of many helpful principles that codependents learn to use through their Twelve-Step meetings. A recent hit song by Mike and the Mechanics, called *"The Living Years,"* speaks of how the clash between our memories and what we desire for today can produce a bitterness that destroys the future. We need to practice letting go of the past and embracing the present.

Let's get back to patience, love, and understanding. Since recovery from drug addiction and, yes, your own recovery from codependency, is going to take some time, let's just take a deep breath and "*Easy Does It*" right into this new way of living, and a new way of thinking. Codependents need to learn how to "detach with love." Before getting into how this is done, let's look at why it is necessary.

ENABLING

Many codependents believe that loving someone means giving the loved one the right to dominate their lives. Parents have been known to "love their children to death"—literally. It is this "smothering" effect—whether by a parent, a spouse, a close friend, teacher, or coworker—that needs to be stopped. Partnerships in work or play, like love, can make you blind—especially when it comes to overlooking the addict's destructive behavior.

If a policeman, for example, begins to develop a drinking problem, and slaps his wife around occasionally, chances are his partners and friends in the police department may cover up for him. In all occupations this cover-up, or "enabling" happens. Almost everyone participates in the cover-up, especially when the problem seems to be relatively harmless and infrequent. "What the hell," they say, "he hasn't tied one on in quite a while, and she probably deserved a slap or two." This type of comment, between friends talking over a beer after work, is not uncommon. Another one we often hear is, "*She can't be an alcoholic; she hasn't had a drink all summer.*" Rationalizations comparing one type of abuse to "worse" types of abuse send cover-up messages, too.

"At least he doesn't use crack. Besides, a lot of people smoke grass. So what?"

Enabling takes the form of making excuses for the abuser, lending money, taking over work responsibilities when necessary, and going even so far as to attend the funeral—except by that time, it's a permanent "cover-up." Often, even an addict's death isn't attributed to the drug use and abuse. The true cause of death gets masked over. But hearts don't just give up; livers don't suddenly shut down. Still, most people shrug it off with, *"So he drank a little; at least he died happy."* If this person had been happy, he or she wouldn't have been putting poisonous chemicals into his or her system to change the normal state of mind.

I've read about differences between American and Japanese attitudes toward enabling. In Japan, some communities simply refuse to accept alcohol and drug abuse within their work force. Workers refuse to cover up for each other's irresponsibilities and immaturities, those which alcohol and drug abuse create. Family members, neighbors, friends on and off the job, and society in general, just do not accept drug addiction. Japan's economic success speaks for itself. It is a testimony to the power of a drug-free culture. By contrast, drug abuse, and the apathy and enabling related to it, have put the arm and leg of America to sleep. Yet some people will insist that there isn't any problem in their immediate home, workplace, school or neighborhood. This is denial speaking. It isn't only the addict who uses denial.

Now that the surface of the problem has been scratched, where does the solution begin? To paraphrase a message Michael Jackson sang around the world in the song, "Man in the Mirror,"—"let it begin with the man in the mirror." *The solution begins with the person you see in the mirror.* But what needs to be changed? Figure 7, on the next page, shows steps leading progressively downward, toward chaos. Read down these steps and note the ones you've travelled before. How have you handled the drug addict or drug user?

First the nagging begins, and then the silent treatment is used to try to control the addict. A surprise visit from someone quickly creates the illusion of a happy household. Even close family friends get confused and torn between loyalties. Children, and sometimes even the household pets, take sides! On the job there is usually dissension, and general disharmony, including back-biting, gossiping (a big clue), and eventually apathy and anger: *"Leave me alone!"* Everyone feels an inability to make decisions. Nothing works. Insanity is at the helm.

Figure 7. Progression of Codependency

The Codependent:

↓ DENIES AND MINIMIZES
"After all, everyone uses some drugs."

  ↓ BEGINS TO CREATE A DREAM WORLD
  Makes up stories and excuses

    ↓ FEELS ABUSED, HURT, GUILTY, ANGRY
    Begins to play childhood tapes of alco-
    holism and family confusions, reliving it.

      ↓ FRANTICALLY PICKS UP PIECES
      Increases enabling. Slow reversal of
      family roles with responsibilities.

        ↓ ACCUSES AND RESENTS LOVED
        ONE
        "If only he/she would listen to me."

          ↓ FEELS DEFEATED, SELF-
          ESTEEM DWINDLES, CHAOS
          BEGINS
          Scared, too.

T.L.C. means "Tender Loving Care" to most people, but to those who suffer from the denial, guilt, anger, and general chaos of codependency sketched above, T.L.C. stands for "Total Lack of Concern." The chaos can become so overwhelming that a state of "*I just don't care anymore*" eventually develops.

SURRENDER

The steps you previously walked down have culminated in what is called "SURRENDER." But surrender to what? To whom? Now it's time to start climbing *up* some steps—all twelve of them. Here's where the Twelve-Step meetings for codependents come in. Local newspapers usually list the Nar-Anon (family and friends of narcotics addicts), Al-Anon (family and friends of alcoholics), Pil-Anon (family and friends of pill addicts) and other family support groups. Your anonymity will be well-protected. Confidentiality is part of the spiritual foundation of all Twelve-Step and Twelve-Tradition programs. There isn't any charge to attend, and if transportation is a problem, call and they'll arrange to pick you up.

All of the books in the world can't replace the healing that takes place at these meetings. If you don't go, you'll never realize this. Remember, they've been there and THEY NEED YOU, too. Don't think about going—just GO!

LETTING GO

"*I can change myself, but I cannot change people, places, or things.*" Now, read that sentence again. Say it aloud. Sing it, chant it, vocalize it at the top of your lungs, until you believe it down to your inner core. "*I CAN CHANGE MYSELF, BUT I CANNOT CHANGE PEOPLE, PLACES, OR THINGS.*" It is almost a God-sent relief when a person grasps this knowledge. You didn't CAUSE your loved one's addiction; you can't CURE it; and you can't CONTROL it . . . but you can definitely CONTRIBUTE to it. Read these four "C"s again.

Another source of comfort and relief is coming to accept that "*The position of God is filled.*" If your response to that is, "*Then why doesn't something get done about (his/her) drug addiction?*"—stop worrying. It will.

Grab this next one with both hands! "*If you're going to worry, then don't pray. If you're going to pray, then don't worry.*" We sometimes lose our two-handed grip on this when we reach down to grab onto a resentment, so avoid reaching for the grudges. Prayer will take the worry away, and it works!

If prayer, and a sense of a loving and forgiving God, is difficult for you (it was for me upon introduction to the Twelve Steps), the loving and caring people at the meetings will act as the necessary Higher Power.

REALISTIC EXPECTATIONS

Much to the surprise of many, there is such a thing as absolutely unacceptable behavior. For instance, no human being, other than a doctor at birth, has the right to hit another person. Nobody, absolutely nobody, should accept physical abuse. Yet some codependents permit themselves to be physically abused by an addict. Usually, both the victim and the aggressor are replaying sick childhood tapes. This means that either their mothers or their fathers had been violent at home—probably seasoned with alcoholism—and they learned to accept physical abuse. If you are the victim of an addict's violent attacks, you must take action. Report this problem to your local mental health agency or department of social services, or phone the police. Modern society has laws against physical abuse, and counseling follows when it is reported.

Let's say I expect the day to be sunny; I expect my mailperson to be on time and to deliver good news; I expect everyone to smile at me; and I expect everything to go my way today. What would you think of this sort of thinking? Just a little wacky, maybe? My expectations of the weather, of the mail coming on time, of everyone smiling (though that is a nice thought), and of everything going my way is silly, agreed? Yet, many people put their expectations out in front of them, and dare anyone to step on them.

Too often, we expect people to read our minds. And when they don't, we're disappointed. For example, a birthday present turns out to be not what you wanted, as though you were convinced you had transferred your request to another's mind without saying anything. There is mental telepathy. I'm not very good at it; are you?

Many people, as they are growing up, create a Cinderella-type story about how they expect their life to turn out. They know exactly what their knight in shining armor will look like, and when he doesn't appear they become terribly disappointed in later years. Many parents do this for their children, planning their kids' entire lives: whom they will date, where they will go to college, what sport they will play, what career they will fulfill, which musical instruments they will become proficient at, how long they will study ballet, and so on and so forth.

This way of thinking by codependents will need much cleaning up. To get started, use this simple image. Did you ever get stuck up in the air on a see-saw when you were a child? When people put their expectations out too far, they get stuck up in the air on the high end of the seesaw. Think of peace of mind as this seesaw. On one side are your expectations, and on the other side, your serenity. When your expectations are too high, your serenity level will go way down into the dirt. But when you lower your expectations, your serenity level begins to rise. You achieve balance—peace of mind. There are millions of people who believe the world is absolutely beautiful. They must be seeing something different than the typical addict. Maybe they are riding high on the serenity side of the seesaw, with their expectations in the dirt.

Your serenity is directly proportional to your level of acceptance. Are you accepting people, places, and things as they are right now? I guess everyone wishes the world were better. But the world is how it is. Stop trying to change it. Instead, try to look at it differently. Try to accept it as it is and change your outlook in relation to it. To begin to see a world that is more beautiful use the "I am . . ." statement for some extra power. Start saying "*I am serene, I am at peace, I am, I am, I am.*" Don't analyze, utilize. Just do it. You'll see some results very shortly. Solutions to many of your problems will follow and reinforce your commitment to improved mental and spiritual health.

COMMUNICATION

Much of the problem of codependency centers on a lack of communication. Different family members, at different times, clam up with expressions like, "Leave me alone," "I've got nothing to say," or "I don't want to talk about it" when in reality they most desperately DO want to talk about it. The irritations and restrained angers have to be released somehow. If suppressed, they will pop, often in unexpected and undesirable ways. The result can be embarrassing and destructive.

The word suppression comes from a Latin word that means to press or squeeze. In English it means to hold back or restrain, to withhold from disclosure. More commonly it means to "stuff it"—farther and farther back. Suppressing your true feelings and reactions to what the addict says or does is guaranteed to destroy communication between you and the addict.

The trouble is you can't always say exactly what you feel either, or the results will be disaster. Sometimes it pays to temporarily stuff a displeasure. How often do we say something like, "Oops, I put my foot in my mouth again." Almost every human being experiences this. One remedy is to remember the slogan *"Put your brain in gear before engaging your mouth."* That has helped many to avoid detonating a family bomb.

Addicts and codependents both have trouble figuring out when it is best to say exactly what they feel and when it is best to hold back. Twelve-Step programs help addicts and codependents learn to make this choice wisely. Family counseling also helps build communication skills. The communication suggestions discussed here are not meant to substitute for professional counseling.

How to Practice Time Out

A technique that has helped many codependents is called "Time Out." "Time Out" is a very simple process for mending hurts and confusions. Time Out is an exercise that a family member can call any time he or she feels bad about what another family member says or does. Time Out requires the participants in the exercise to give their complete, undivided attention to each other. That means no telephone interruptions, the T.V. and radio are off, or in another room where they don't interfere, and all other possible distractions are blocked.

The best location for Time Out is at the kitchen table, where people can sit across from each other. Whichever family member called Time Out will be the first to speak, and the other person will just listen. This person may talk for five minutes, or an hour and five minutes. The other family member must say nothing at all. No questions may be asked of others by the speaker, either. The content of what is said may be right, wrong, or indifferent. That doesn't matter. Suppression is being avoided—and that DOES matter.

When the speaker is finished, he or she says, "And now I'm finished." The one who called Time Out now remains quiet and the opposite person may speak, under the same guidelines as before. This person may talk on and on, but must not be interrupted for any reason at all. The same undivided attention given the first speaker is now returned. Sometimes laughing and even crying occur spontaneously during Time Out sessions, but this is not to be confused with interruptions. Participants are allowed to cry or laugh naturally and appropriately during the exercise. When composure returns, continue the Time Out.

This exercise should not be seen as punishment —just the opposite. After the garbage is removed, compliments and other expressions of sympathy and closeness will follow. But first, you must get to know each other, and Time Out, if practiced as suggested, will help you do just that.

When the second person has concluded with the same words, " . . . and now I'm finished," both participants get up from the table and go in opposite directions, so to speak—temporarily getting away from each other. One may want to do the dishes and the other may want to mow the yard or do other household chores. The point is to reflect carefully on what the other loved one said—what REALLY was said.

Many people who have used the Time Out technique have achieved astonishing results in only a few sessions. The trick is to keep on doing it. Eventually, most people figure out that it is best to call a Time Out before someone blows up—before tempers burst. Actually, God has been very good to us by giving us a built-in alarm system that signals when we're about to get into trouble. There are many names for this, but essentially it's when the adrenaline begins to pump through our system before a blast of anger. This alarm is telling us that we have to make a decision. Are we going to react in a burst of anger, or use this energy to solve the problem? It's valuable energy. Use it; don't just throw it away to another in rage. Use it to solve the problem. Understand, there is always—repeat, always—a solution. Remember that acknowledging a problem is sometimes a solution. By now you realize *you aren't losing your temper, you're losing your valuable energy.*

Some expressed irritations may result in immediate change in the other person's behavior. Some behaviors may never change, although "never" is a strong word. Just keep talking about the things that bother you in the ongoing Time Out sessions. Don't let them build up again.

Time Out participants agree that a minimum of three times a week is a good beginning for getting to know the others you live with. Once the big problems are unloaded in the Time Outs, then the little ones get talked about and most of them removed. So often it is the smaller, insignificant hassles that grind away at us. Yet often the other person isn't aware of these minor irritations.

Some people ask, "Is it okay to have more than one Time Out in one day?" The best answer to this question is "No." More than one Time Out per day would probably interfere with benefiting from the previous one. Let the session filter for the remainder of the day, and talk it through again the following day. If you need to talk about the subject more after the Time Out, call your sponsor and discuss any confusions. (And yes, sponsorship is available to family members, too.) If confusion persists, go to a meeting.

This discussion of communication began with the idea of avoiding suppression. So much of drug addiction involves the use of suppressants (chemicals that suppress an action, reaction or appetite). The very word darkens any hope of mending the pieces. Take off the blanket of suppression, and communicate!

Communication involves active listening, not just hearing. *Are you prepared to listen to the addict's message? Have you tried listening to what he or she ISN'T saying?*

HOW TO AVOID STEALING THE RESPONSIBILITY

God, grant me the
Serenity to accept the people I cannot change;
Courage to change the person I can; and the
Wisdom to know it's me!

Part of the dis-EASE of codependency is trying constantly to solve problems for others. An important consideration in learning how to stop being the antidote for the addict's pain is to keep the responsibility where it belongs. Your loved one's recovery from drug addiction is not your responsibility. While the disease is active, if more codependents would stop picking up the pieces—stealing responsibility from the addict—recovery would occur sooner for more people.

Don't misunderstand me. I am not talking about your responsibility to report dangerous and life-threatening behavior—that is the responsibility of all members of society. I once reported a state policeman to his superior; the policeman was driving dangerously—drunkenly—while on duty. That same policeman is enjoying sobriety today. A friend reported a doctor with a cocaine abuse problem to the physician's impairment committee. That doctor in turn got help. This is not what I mean by taking the responsibility away from the drug addict or the alcoholic. It is just the opposite: it is fulfilling society's responsibility.

Reflecting Back Responsibility

Let's say the addict/alcoholic (whether in recovery or not) asks for some advice from you. Remember, part of YOUR illness is always trying to solve others' problems. What should you say? Think of a tennis court, with a net between you and the addict. Your purpose will be to keep the "ball"—the responsibility—on the addict's side of the net. Whatever the problem you're being asked to solve, try to reply with something like, "Okay, I understand. So what are you going to do about it?" That keeps the ball on the addict's side of the court, where it belongs.

Your reply might immediately take hold, and the addict will begin to solve the problem. On the other hand, he or she might throw the ball back over to your side of the net by saying, "Well, that's why I'm asking you." Now you've got the ball again; push it back. You say, "So what do you think you'd want to do about it, if you could?" Now the ball is back over on the addict's side of the net again. Be sure to keep your voice low and remain calm. Avoid threatening or indifferent facial expressions, and never let sarcasm into your tone of voice. Keep this up, and watch how the addict begins to take more responsibility for his life.

Later, the recovering addict will need to know this secret way of dealing with newcomers, to have more success in sponsoring other addicts. But for now, just practice it without describing the outcome or the purpose. It will be difficult, at first, because often you may have the correct answer. But as long as there are people picking up the pieces ("enablers") and taking the responsibility away from where it belongs, there will be no improvements. *Practice makes progress.*

A Final Word

I sincerely hope that you, the reader, realize by now that recovery isn't a matter of luck or magic. A person doesn't simply reach out and grab dignity, happiness, love, integrity and self-esteem. These valued qualities and good feelings result from a drug-free lifestyle that involves Learning to Live Again. They are an outgrowth of new choices supported by a strong desire to leave behind the daily hell that all of us addicts somehow barely managed to exit in.

When I originally came into recovery, I hadn't planned to stay this long. Then I realized, "I am worth it." And you are worth it. Whatever it takes, we can do it together! Recovery in a Twelve-Step program will take all the fight we still have in us. But if we put just one-half of the energy into recovery that we used to support our addiction, we will be assured a successful journey into a clean, sober and rewarding life—being a winner. I have heard many addicts say that their worst day in recovery, being clean, was far better than their best day of active drug addiction.

I sincerely hope that after reading this book and thinking about the ideas I have shared, you will be inspired to try this new way of life. Remember: *Just for Today* and, *One Day at a Time* is how we stay drug free and truly learn to live again.

I welcome letters from anyone who wants to write to me, at the address noted in the front of this book, just to let me know how your recovery is going.

You are a winner . . . today!

Appendix

HELP FOR OTHER ADDICTIONS

Many drug addicts who seek help realize their powerlessness over other addictions. Listed below are other self-help resources.

Adult Children of Alcoholics
Central Service Board
P.O. Box 3216
Torrance, CA 90505

Al-Anon/Alateen Family Group Headquarters
Madison Square Station
New york, NY 10010
(212) 683-1771

Alcoholics Anonymous
World Service Office
468 Park Avenue South
New York, NY 10016
(212) 686-1100

Cocaine Anonymous World Services
P.O. Box 1367
Culver City, CA 90232
(213) 559-5833

Co-Dependents Anonymous
P.O. Box 33577
Phoenix, AZ 85067-3577
(602) 944-0141

Debtors Anonymous
P.O. Box 20322
New York, NY 10025-9992

Emotions Anonymous
P.O. Box 4245
St. Paul, MN 55104

Gamblers Anonymous
P.O. Box 17173
Los Angeles, CA 90017

Narcotics Anonymous
World Service Office
16155 Wyandotte Street
Van Nuys, CA 91406
(818) 780-3951

National Clearinghouse for Alcohol Information
P.O. Box 1908
Rockville, MD 20850
(301) 468-2600

Overeaters Anonymous
World Service Office
2190 190th Street
Torrance, CA 90504
(213) 320-7941

Sexaholics Anonymous
P.O. Box 300
Simi Valley, CA 93062
(805) 581-3343